Arthur Asa Berger

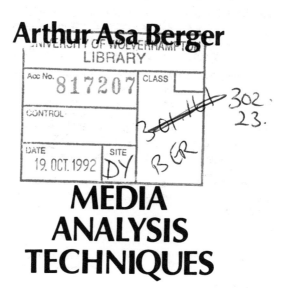

MEDIA
ANALYSIS
TECHNIQUES

Revised Edition

Volume 10   **The Sage COMMTEXT Series**

SAGE PUBLICATIONS
The International Professional Publishers
Newbury Park   London   New Delhi

For information address:

SAGE Publications, Inc.
2455 Teller Road
Newbury Park, California 91320

SAGE Publications Ltd.
6 Bonhill Street
London EC2A 4PU
United Kingdom

SAGE Publications India Pvt. Ltd.
M-32 Market
Greater Kailash I
New Delhi 110 048 India

Printed in the United States of America

Library of Congress Cataloging-in-Publication Data

Berger, Arthur Asa, 1933-
     Media analysis techniques / Arthur Asa Berger. — Rev. ed.
          p.   cm. — (The Sage commtext series ; v. 10)
     Includes bibliographical references and index.
     ISBN 0-8039-4361-X. — ISBN 0-8039-4362-8 (pb)
     1. Mass media—Methodology. 2. Mass media criticism. I. Title.
     II. Series.
     P91.B43   1991
     302.23′01—dc20   91-15067
                                                                 CIP

92 93 94 15 14 13 12 11 10 9 8 7 6 5 4 3

Sage Production Editor: Astrid Virding

*This book is dedicated
to my colleagues in the
Broadcast Communication Arts Department,
and to my students.*

CONTENTS

ACKNOWLEDGMENTS

My thanks to: Groucho Marx, Karl Marx, Sigmund Freud, Fustel de Coulanges, Roland Barthes, Umberto Eco, Agostino Lombardo, Giuseppe Gadda-Conti, Jean-Marie Benoist, George Gerbner, Dave Noble, Marshall McLuhan, Michael Real, Vladimir Propp, Ernest Dichter, Claude Lévi-Strauss, William Fry, Jr., Bronislaw Malinowski, Ferdinand de Saussure, Johan Huizinga, Joe Meeker, Irving Louis Horowitz, Jason Berger, Jonathan Culler, Stanley Milgram, Mircea Eliade, John Cawelti, Cecilia Bartholomew, Henri Lefebvre, Elihu Katz, Daniel Dayan, Mike Noll, Peter Clarke, Ev Dennis, Howard and Barbara Ginsberg, Isaac Silberman, Ron Compesi, Howard Rheingold, Conrad Kottak, Asa Briggs, Tony Fellow, Tom Inge, Jeremy Klein, Raphael Patai, Mary Douglas, Bruno Bettelheim, David Manning White, Orrin Klapp, Warren Bennis, Tom and Bella Clougher, Alan Dundes, Brom Weber, Mulford Q. Sibley, Lauri Honko, Jean Guenot, Randy Harrison, Claude Cossette, and Stan Lee. My chapter on semiological/semiotic analysis (Chapter 1) appeared, in slightly modified form, in *Understanding Television: Essays on Television as a Social and Cultural Force,* edited by Richard P. Adler. Special thanks to Aaron Wildavsky, for his sage counsel, and to F. Gerald Kline, for his editorial advice.

PREFACE TO REVISED EDITION

It is a great pleasure for me to write a preface to the revised edition of this book. *Media Analysis Techniques* was published in 1982, so it is almost ten years between editions. Ten years and eleven printings. And an Italian version, *Tecniche di analisi dei mass media,* published by ERI/Edizioni Rai Radiotelevisione Italiana, as well.

I think *Media Analysis Techniques* has achieved its modest success because it empowers its readers. There are, I believe, two fundamental ways to teach media criticism. One way is ask students to read critical essays and discuss the content of these essays . . . and, perhaps, deal with the methodology employed by the writers. The other way is to focus on methods: teach students methodologies and give the students an opportunity to apply the methodologies to television programs, films, advertisements and various other texts. My book takes the methodological approach, though in the second half of the book I offer a number of essays which show how the four techniques discussed in the first part of the book can be applied.

Popular culture changes so rapidly that just about any film or television series you deal with becomes part of what my students see as "ancient history." Therefore, I chose topics for the applications section that won't get outdated: a classic detective story (which was made into a very fine film), football (with a focus on how it is presented on television), magazine advertising, and all-news radio.

I have made a moderate number of additions to the chapters. For the most part I have added new concepts to the methodology chapters and amplified my discussion of certain topics that I felt needed more elaboration. The subjects I deal with in the first half of the book, semiology/semiotics, psychoanalytic criticism, Marxist theory and sociological criticism are all enormously complex and each have been the subjects of endless numbers of articles and books. (*Media Analysis Techniques* is a thin book that could easily become a very fat book . . . or four very fat books.) What I have tried to do, in each discussion, is focus upon concepts that help us understand texts and the mass media. I chose these four methodologies because I think they are of paramount importance, but there are many other approaches that could have been taken. I discuss this subject in the epilogue of the book.

I hope that this edition of *Media Analysis Techniques* helps readers better understand the four methodologies discussed and that this little book will help readers gain enough understanding of the techniques discussed so they can become their own media analysts. I have added some new sources to the bibliographies at the end of each chapter and have also added an index.

PREFACE

Imagine, if you will, a room in which four people are sitting, watching the episode of *Dallas* in which J.R. Ewing is shot. The four people are television critics, each for one of the following magazines: *Marxist Critical Studies of Media, Psychoanalysis and the Public Arts, Sign: Semiological Inquiries into Popular Culture,* and *Media and Society.* None of these magazines exists, as far as I know, but publications like them do.

After watching the program, each critic writes a review suitable for his or her publication. The Marxist critic dwells on the degradation of the characters and shows how each is alienated, reflecting the horrors of bourgeois capitalist societies in general and America in particular. *Dallas,* then, is an unwitting exposé of the moral degeneracy and corruption found in all bourgeois capitalist societies. The psychoanalytically oriented critic explains that *Dallas* is *really* about the Oedipal problems of J.R., which are unresolved, and his sibling rivalry with Bobby. J.R.'s behavior is best explained, then, using psychoanalytic concepts. J.R. has no superego or conscience and this is tied, ultimately, to his relationship with his mother. The semiological critic would focus attention on how meaning is generated in the program—on the significance of Southfork and the Ewing tower, J.R.'s overdrawn facial expressions, the spatiality of the sets, and everything else that is done to give viewers the ideas and feelings that the writers, actors, and directors want the audience to have. And the sociological critic would focus on the various roles the characters have, the fact that certain social groupings are underrepresented (or not represented) in the program, and the different gratifications that members of the audience get from watching the program.

After reading this book you should be able to write all four of these types of reviews. The first section of the book is made up of chapters that introduce semiological, psychoanalytic (Freudian), Marxist, and sociological thought. These chapters should be read as "primers" that discuss some of the more important concepts in each domain. An annotated bibliography is provided at the end of each of these chapters, to assist the reader in finding useful books in each area.

The second section of the book consists of essays that demonstrate how the various perspectives might be applied to the public arts. Thus you will find chapters on *Murder on the Orient Express,* fashion and cosmetic advertising in *Vogue,* football, and all-news radio stations that use the techniques explained in the first part of the book.

I hope you will find this volume informative and entertaining, and that it will help you to see the public arts and popular culture in new and interesting ways.

—*Arthur Asa Berger*
Mill Valley, California

I

TECHNIQUES OF INTERPRETATION

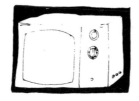

1

SEMIOLOGICAL ANALYSIS

Semiology—the science of signs—is concerned, primarily, with how meaning is generated in "texts" (films, television programs, and other works of art). It deals with what signs are and how they function. In this chapter, after discussing the most essential semiological concepts and some related concerns, we apply them to an episode of a television program. We then deal with codes, formulas, and the "language" of television.

I face this assignment—explaining semiology and showing how it can be applied to television and popular culture to those who know little or nothing about the subject—with a certain amount of apprehension. I'm not sure whether semiology (also sometimes called semiotics) is a subject, a movement, a philosophy, or a cult-like religion. I do know that there is a large and rapidly expanding literature on the subject and that many of the writings by semiologists are difficult and highly technical.

So my mission, if not impossible, is quite challenging. For not only am I to explain the fundamental notions or elements of semiology, I am also to apply them to television and television productions as well as to popular culture in general. It is a large undertaking, but I think it can be done.

The price I must pay involves a certain amount of simplification and narrowness of focus. I'm going to explain the basic principles of semiology and apply them. I hope that after reading this chapter and the annotated bibliography provided, those interested in the matter can probe more deeply into it at their own convenience.

A BRIEF HISTORY OF THE SUBJECT

Although an interest in signs and the way they communicate has a long history (medieval philosophers, John Locke, and others have shown interest), modern semiological analysis can be said to have begun with two men—Swiss linguist Ferdinand de Saussure (1857-1913) and American philosopher Charles Saunders Peirce (1839-1914).[1]

Saussure's book, *Course in General Linguistics*, first published posthumously in 1915, suggests the possibility of semiological analysis. It deals with many of the concepts that can be applied to signs and that are explicated in this essay. Saussure's division of the sign into two components, the signifier, or "sound-image," and the signified, or "concept," and his suggestions that the relationship between signifiers and signified is arbitrary were of crucial importance for the development of semiology. Peirce, on the other hand, focused on three aspects of signs—their iconic, indexical, and symbolic dimensions (see Figure 1.1).

From these two points of departure a movement was born, and semiological analysis (I will use that term exclusively, henceforth) has spread all over the globe. Important work was done in Prague and Russia early in the twentieth century, and semiology is now well established in France and Italy (where Roland Barthes, Umberto Eco, and many others are doing important theoretical as well as applied work). There are also outposts of progress in England, the United States, and many other countries.

Semiology has been applied, with interesting results, to film, theatre, medicine, architecture, zoology, and a host of other areas that involve or are concerned with communication and the transfer of information. In fact, some semiologists, perhaps carried away with things, suggest that *everything* can be analyzed semiologically; they see it as the queen of the interpretive sciences, the key that unlocks the meaning of all things great and small.

Peirce argued that interpreters had to supply part of the meaning of signs. He wrote that a sign "is something which stands to somebody for something in some respect or capacity." This is different from Saussure's ideas about how signs function. Peirce considered

	Icon	Index	Symbol
signify by	resemblance	causal connections	conventions
examples	pictures, statues	smoke/fire, symptoms/disease	words, numbers, flags
process	can see	can figure out	must learn

Figure 1.1. Three Aspects of Signs

semiotics important because, as he puts it, "this universe is perfused with signs, if it is not composed exclusively of signs." Whatever we do can be seen as a message, or as Peirce would put it, a sign. If everything in the universe is a sign, semiotics becomes extremely important, if not all-important (a view that both semioticians and semiologists, whatever their disagreements, support wholeheartedly).

Whether this is the case is questionable, but without doubt semiology has been used by all kinds of people in interesting ways. It has only recently been taken seriously in the United States, however, and is still not widely used or taught here. There are several reasons for this. First, we tend to be pragmatic and down to earth, and abstruse, theoretical, and formalistic methodologies are not congenial to us. Also, there is a kind of international cultural lag that exists; it takes a while for movements that are important in the European intellectual scene to become accepted, let alone popular, in the United States. It was the French who "discovered" Faulkner and film (as a significant art form) and, though important work was done here by Peirce, as I mentioned earlier, we had to wait for semiological analysis to evolve and mature in Europe before it caught our attention here.

THE PROBLEM OF MEANING

In what follows we are going to be learning a new language—a number of concepts that enable us to look at films, television programs, fashion, foods—almost anything—in ways somewhat different from the manner in which we generally look at these things. *Our basic concern will always be how meaning is generated and conveyed,* with particular reference to the films or television programs we will be examining. (Henceforth we will focus on television programs, which will be called "texts.")

But how is meaning generated?

The essential breakthrough of semiology is to take linguistics as a model and apply linguistic concepts to other phenomena—texts—and not just to language itself. In fact, we treat texts as being like languages, in that relationships are all important, and not things per se. To quote Jonathan Culler:

> The notion that linguistics might be useful in studying other cultural phenomena is based on two fundamental insights: first, that social and cultural phenomena are not simply material objects or events but objects or events with meaning, and hence signs; and second, that they do not have essences but are defined by a network of relations. (1976: 4)

Signs and relations! They are two of the key notions of semiological analysis. A text such as *Star Trek* can be thought of as a system of signs, and the meaning in the program stems from the signs and from the system that ties the signs together. This system is generally not obvious and must be elicited from the text.

In semiological analysis we make an arbitrary and temporary separation of content and form and focus our attention on the system of signs that makes up a text. Thus a meal, to stray from television for a moment, is not seen as steak, salad, baked potato, and apple pie, but rather as a sign system conveying meanings related to matters such as status, taste, sophistication, nationality, and so on.

Perhaps it is best now to quote from one of the founding fathers of semiology, Swiss linguist Ferdinand de Saussure:

> Language is a system of signs that express ideas, and is therefore comparable to a system of writing, the alphabet of deaf-mutes, symbolic rites, polite formulas, military signals, etc. But it is the most important of all these systems.
>
> *A science that studies the life of signs within society* is conceivable; it would be a part of social psychology and consequently of general psychology; I shall call it *semiology* (from Greek *semeion* "sign"). Semiology would show what constitutes signs, what laws govern them. Since the science does not yet exist, no one can say what it would be; but it has a right to existence, a place staked out in advance. (1966: 16)

This is the charter statement of semiology, a statement that opens the study of media to us, for not only can we study symbolic rites and military signals, we can also study commercials, soap operas, situation comedies, and almost anything else as "sign systems."

Saussure offered another crucial insight that is relevant here—that concepts have meaning because of relations and the basic relationship is oppositional. Thus "rich" doesn't mean anything unless there is "poor," or "happy" unless there is "sad." "Concepts are purely differential and defined not by their positive content but negatively by their relations with the other terms of the system" (Saussure, 1966: 117). It is not "content" that determines meaning, but "relations" in some kind of a system. The "most precise characteristic" of these concepts "is in being what the others are not" (Saussure, 1966: 117). We can see this readily enough in language, but it also holds for texts. Nothing has meaning in itself!

One thing we must remember when thinking about oppositions is that the opposing concepts must be related in some way. There is always some topic (not always mentioned) that they deal with. For example: rich/WEALTH/poor or happy/MENTAL STATE/sad. I wrote an article, a number of years ago, in which I discussed blue jeans and what I called the "denimization" phenomenon and contrasted it with fancy clothes. Some of the differences are listed below, with the topic dealt with printed in all caps:

DENIM		*FANCY CLOTHES*
cheap	COST	expensive
rough	TEXTURE	smooth
mass produced	FABRICATION	hand made
department stores	PLACE BOUGHT	boutiques

If you cannot find a subject that the oppositional terms relate to, there is probably something wrong with them.

So where are we now? I have suggested that semiological analysis is concerned with meaning in texts, that meaning stems from relationships, and, in particular, the relationship among signs. But what, exactly, is a sign?

SIGNS

A sign, Saussure tells us, is a combination of a concept and a sound-image, a combination that cannot be separated. But because these terms are not quite satisfactory for him he modifies them slightly:

I propose to retain the word sign [signe] to designate the whole and to replace concept and sound-image respectively by *signified* [signifié] and *signifier* [signifiant]; the last two terms have the advantage of indicating the opposition that separates them from each other and from the whole of which they are parts. (Saussure, 1966: 67)

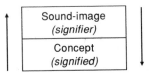

Figure 1.2. Saussure's Diagram of a Sign

The relationship between the signifier and signified—and this is crucial—is *arbitrary,* unmotivated, un-natural. There is no logical connection between a word and a concept or a signifier and signified, a point that makes finding meaning in texts interesting and problematical.

Saussure uses trees as an example. He offers a diagram of the sign in general (see Figure 1.2), and then of the *sign* tree (Figure 1.3).

The difference between a sign and a symbol, Saussure suggests, is that a symbol has a signifier that is never wholly arbitrary.

> One characteristic of the symbol is that it is never wholly arbitrary; it is not empty, for there is a rudiment of a natural bond between the signifier and signified. The symbol of justice, a pair of scales, could not be replaced by just another symbol, such as a chariot. (1966: 68)

We now can start looking at texts differently and can start thinking about how it is that signifiers generate meaning.

How do signifiers generate meaning? And how is it that we know these meanings? If the relationship between a signifier and signified is arbitrary, the meanings these signifiers hold must be learned somehow, which implies that there are certain structured associations, or *codes,* we pick up that help us interpret signs. (I will deal with this subject in more detail shortly.)

Let's look at the television program *Star Trek* in terms of its signifiers and what is signified. Anyone who has seen the program knows that it is a space adventure/science fiction series. We know this because we are "told" so at the beginning of each episode, when the Starship Enterprise is sent on a mission in outer space—to explore new worlds and seek out new civilizations, to "boldly go where no man has gone before." We can say that science fiction adventure is the general "signified" and that numbers of signifiers are given to show this. For example, we find rocket ships, futuristic uniforms, ray guns, advanced computer technology, extraterrestrials with strange powers (such as Mr. Spock, whose pointy ears signify that he is only partly human), and magic/science, among other things.

It is precisely the fact that the program is so rich in signifiers that enables the legions of "Trekkies" to hold conventions, wear costumes,

Figure 1.3. Saussure's Diagram of the Sign and Symbol "Tree"

sell "phasers," and so on. For when you have appropriated the signifiers, you have "captured," so to speak, the signified. This, I might point out, is how many commercials work. People purchase the "right" products and assume (or hope) that these products will signify a certain social class, status, lifestyle, or what you will.

All of this is based on associations we learn and then carry around with us. Anyone who communicates uses these associations between signifiers and signifieds all the time. Since in real life the relationships are arbitrary and change rapidly, one must be on one's toes all the time. Signifiers can become dated and change their significance all too quickly. In a sense, then, we are all practicing semiologists who pay a great deal of attention to signs—signifiers and signifieds—even though we may never have heard these terms before.

Many of us have followed the adventures of a detective who was (like all the classical detectives) a first class semiologist—though we were unaware of this because we didn't know about the existence of semiology. I am talking about Sherlock Holmes. Inevitably there is some situation that arises that puzzles everyone, which Holmes then "solves." He does this by reading signs which others ignore as trivial and inconsequential. In one story, "The Blue Carbuncle," Watson finds Holmes examining a hat that had been brought to him by a policeman. Watson describes the hat: it was old, its lining was discolored, it was cracked, very dusty and spotted in places. Holmes asks Watson what he can deduce from the hat about its wearer. Watson examines the hat and says he can deduce nothing.

Holmes then proceeds to describe, in remarkable detail, what the man who owned the hat is like. He is, Holmes says: highly intellectual, has had a decline in fortune, his wife no longer loves him, he is sedentary, and probably doesn't have gas in his house. Watson exclaims, "You are certainly joking, Holmes." Holmes then shows Watson how he reached his conclusions. He examined the hat, noticed certain things about it (signifiers) and proceeded from there (described the implied signifieds).

SIGN	
signifier Sound-image	*signified* Concept

Figure 1.4.

Signifiers	*Signifieds*
Cubic capacity of hat (large brain)	Man is intellectual
Good quality hat but three years old	Man hasn't a new hat, suggesting a decline in fortune
Hat hasn't been brushed in weeks	Man's wife no longer loves him
Dust on hat is brown housedust	Man seldom goes out
Wax stains from candles on hat	No gas in house

Holmes explains Watson's mistake. "*You fail . . . to reason from what you see. You are too timid in drawing your inferences.*" Watson had said that he saw nothing in the hat. What he did was to fail to recognize the signifiers he examined for what they were. This failure is common in readers of detective novels, who pass over vital information, not recognizing it for what it is. Some semiologists are, on the other hand, not timid enough in drawing their inferences, but that is another matter. *The meaning in signs, and texts (which can be looked upon as collections of signs) is not always (or even often) evident; it has to be elicited.* And too many people are like Watson, I would suggest—not bold enough in drawing their inferences.

SIGNS AND TRUTH

Umberto Eco has suggested that if signs can be used to tell the truth, they can also be used to lie. He writes in *A Theory of Semiotics*:

Semiotics is concerned with everything that can be taken as a sign. A sign is everything which can be taken as significantly substituting for something else. This something else does not necessarily have to exist or to actually be somewhere at the moment in which a sign stands for it. Thus semiotics is in principle the discipline studying everything which can be used in order to lie. If something cannot be used to tell a lie, conversely it cannot be used to tell the truth; it cannot be used "to tell" at all. I think that the definition of a "theory of the lie" should be taken as a pretty comprehensive program for a general semiotics. (1976: 7)

Let us consider some ways that we can (and do) lie, or, to be kinder, mislead others with signs.

Area	Misleading Signs
Wigs	Bald person or with different hair color
Elevator Shoes	Short person made taller
Dyed hair	Blondes are really brunettes, etc. etc.
Falsies	Women with small breasts seem to have big ones
Imposters	Pretend to be doctors, lawyers, etc.
Impersonation	Pretend to be someone else,, steal "identity"
Malingering	Pretend to be ill
Theatre	Pretend to have feelings, beliefs, etc.
Food	Imitation crab, shrimp, lobster, etc.
Words	White lies told so as not to hurt people

We live in a world full of signs that lie and mislead and many of us spend a good deal of effort trying to determine whether or not we are being "conned." Much of this lying with signs is relatively harmless (the blondes who are naturally brunettes) but in some cases (the truck driver who pretends to be a doctor) it could be very dangerous. Eco's point is an important one—if signs can be used to communicate, they can be used to communicate lies.

LANGUAGE AND SPEAKING

Earlier I suggested that texts (such as films, television programs, commercials, and so on) are "like languages," and that the rules of linguistics can be applied to them. What languages do is enable us to communicate information, feelings, ideas, and the like by establishing systems and rules that people learn. And just as there is grammar for writing and speaking, there is also a grammar for various kinds of texts—and for different media.

Saussure made a distinction that is useful here—between *language* and *speaking*. Language is a social institution, made up of rules and conventions that have been systematized, that enables us to speak (or, more broadly, communicate). Each person "speaks" in his or her own manner, but this speaking is based on the language and rules that everyone learns. A television program such as *Star Trek*—and I must point out that most of what I'm dealing with involves narratives—can be looked upon as speech that is intelligible to its audience because the audience knows the language. That is, we know the signs and what they signify, we know the conventions of the genre or what is acceptable and unacceptable. We know the codes!

Sometimes there is confusion and the code of the creator of a program isn't the code of the members of the audience. In such cases there is bad communication. What makes things complicated is the fact that, *generally speaking, people are not consciously aware of the rules and codes and cannot articulate them,* though they respond to them. A scene in a program that is meant to be sad but which occasions laughter is an example of this kind of mix-up.

It is obvious, then, that people are "speaking" all the time, even when they aren't saying anything. Our hairstyles, eyeglasses, clothes, facial expressions, posture, gestures, and many other things about us are communicating or "speaking" (that is, signifying continually, for those who are sensitive to such things and who are mindful of signs and signifiers). In an article titled "How They Know What You Really Mean," Maya Pines offers an explanation of semiotics:

> Everything we do sends messages about us in a variety of codes, semiologists contend. We are also on the receiving end of innumerable messages encodeed in music, gestures, foods, rituals, books, movies, or advertisements. Yet we seldom realize that we have received such messages, and would have trouble explaining the rules under which they operate. (*San Francisco Chronicle,* Oct. 13, 1982)

What semiotics does, she adds, is teach us how to decipher these rules and "bring them to consciousness." I have described the messages we give and receive as being similar to "speech." Speech always implies, as Saussure (1966) tells us, an established system, though this system is also evolving continually.

Let me offer a brief summary here:

(1) Our concern is how *meaning* is created and conveyed in texts and, in particular, narratives (or stories).

(2) Our focus is upon the *signs* we find in these texts, understanding signs to be combinations of *signifiers* and signifieds.

(3) Since nothing has meaning in itself, the *relationships* that exist among signs are crucial. An analogy can be made with words and grammar here; it is the way the words are combined that determines what they mean. *Language* is a social institution that tells us how words are to be used and *speaking* is an individual act based on language.

(4) *Texts* can be looked upon as being similar to speech and implying grammars or languages that make these texts meaningful. There are codes

and conventions that make the signs in a narrative understandable and that also shape the actions.

THE SYNCHRONIC AND THE DIACHRONIC

This distinction is yet another legacy from Saussure. As he uses the terms, "synchronic" means analytical and "diachronic" means historical, so a synchronic study of a text looks at the relationships that exists among its elements and a diachronic study looks at the way the narrative evolves. Another way of putting this is that a synchronic analysis of a text looks for the pattern of paired oppositions buried in the text (the paradigmatic structure) while a diachronic analysis focuses upon the chain of events (the syntagmatic structure) that forms the narrative.

Figure 1.5 shows these relationships more clearly. Claude Lévi-Strauss and Vladimir Propp are offered here as exemplars of each method. Their ideas will be explained in the sections that follow.

SYNTAGMATIC ANALYSIS

A syntagm is a chain, and a syntagmatic analysis of a text looks at it as a sequence of events that forms some kind of a narrative. I will be dealing with the ideas of a Russian folklorist, Vladimir Propp, who wrote a pioneering book in 1928, *Morphology of the Folktale*. Morphology is the study of forms—that is, the component parts of something and their relationships to each other and to the whole.

Propp did his work on a group of fairy tales and describes his method as follows:

> We are undertaking a comparison of the themes of these tales. For the sake of comparison we shall separate the component parts of fairy tales by special methods; and then, we shall make a comparison of the tales according to their components. The result will be a morphology (i.e., a description of the tale according to its component parts and the relationship of these components to each other and to the whole). (1968: 19)

The essential or basic narrative unit that Propp (1968: 21-23) used was what he called a "function."

> *Function is understood as an act of a character, defined from the point of view of its significance for the course of the action.*

SYNCHRONIC	DIACHRONIC
simultaneity	succession
static	evolutionary
relations in a system	relations in time
paradigmatic	syntagmatic
Lévi-Strauss	Propp

Figure 1.5. Elements of Synchronic Analysis and Diachronic Analysis

The observations cited may be briefly formulated in the following manner:

(1) *Functions of characters serve as stable, constant elements in a tale, independent of how and by whom they are fulfilled. They constitute the fundamental components of a tale.*

(2) *The number of functions known to the fairy tale is limited.*

(3) *The sequence of functions is always identical.*

(4) *All fairy tales are of one type in regard to their structure.*

Propp's work has great significance to us, for we can adopt and adapt his ideas to films, television stories, comics, and all kinds of other narratives. Whether or not Propp was correct in all his assertions is not of great importance to us here. His concept of functions can be applied to all kinds of texts with interesting results.

Propp gives a summary of the essence of each function, an abbreviated definition of it in one word, and a conventional sign for it. Some functions are rather complicated and have numerous subcategories, all of which fulfill the same task.

Propp's first function is quoted below so that you can see what a simple one is like and how he develops each:

(I) ONE OF THE MEMBERS OF A FAMILY ABSENTS HIMSELF FROM HOME. (Definition: *absentation*. Designation: β.)

    (1) *The person absenting himself can be a member of the older generation* (β_1). Parents leave for work (113). "The prince had to go on a distant journey, leaving his wife to the care of strangers" (265). "Once, he (a merchant) went away to foreign lands" (17). Usual forms of absentation: going to work, to the forest, to trade, to war, "on business."

    (2) *An intensified form of absentation is represented by the death of parents* (β_2).

(3) *Sometimes members of the younger generation absent themselves* (β_3). They go visiting (101), fishing (108), for a walk (137), out to gather berries (244) [Propp, 1968: 26; the numbers in parentheses refer to specific fairy tales studied by Propp].

This is one of Propp's briefer functions; for instance, number 8 (about a villain doing harm or injury to a member of a family) has 19 subcategories.

Even though we do not possess all the subcategories of each function, it is still possible to use Propp's 31 functions to make syntagmatic analyses of selected texts (Figure 1.6 presents these functions and a brief description of each). What will become obvious to you as you use these functions is the degree to which many contemporary stories contain many of Propp's functions. His definition of the hero as "that character who either directly suffers from the action of the villain . . . or who agrees to liquidate the misfortune or lack of another person" is also worth considering (Propp, 1968: 50). Heroes also, he tells us, are supplied with magical agents or helpers that they make use of in difficult situations.

Figure 1.6 (which contains a simplification and slight modification of Propp's list) gives each function and describes it briefly.

I will now apply Propp's functions to an episode of the television program *The Prisoner* to show how Propp helps us uncover the morphology of a narrative text. *The Prisoner* is a remarkable "existential" television series first broadcast a number of years ago. It is regarded by many people as a classic. It is about a spy who resigns from some mysterious organization, returns to his apartment, where he is gassed, and then wakes up in a strange, resort-like, island prison, the Village, where everyone is called by a number. The hero, "the prisoner," is locked into battles with various adversaries, each playing Number Two, in the 17 episodes of the series. At the end of the series, the prisoner (Number Six) escapes from the Village, which he destroys, and returns to his apartment in London.

A synopsis of the first episode, "Arrival," follows:

The program opens with a scene in which the hero, unnamed, is shown resigning. He is in an office with some officials; he pounds the table and leaves. He returns to his apartment and begins packing. As he does this, he is gassed and passes out. He wakes in the Village, a resort-like prison (and a totalitarian society) where everyone has numbers instead of names. He is told that he is Number Six and is pitted against Number Two, who wishes to find out why Six resigned. Six tries to escape by running along the seashore but is "captured" by a huge and terrifying rubber sphere, Rover,

α	*Initial situation*	Members of family or hero introduced.
β	*Absentation*	One of the members of the family absents himself from home.
γ	*Interdiction*	An interdiction is addressed to the hero.
δ	*Violation*	An interdiction is violated.
ε	*Reconnaissance*	The villain makes an attempt at reconnaissance.
η	*Delivery*	The villain receives information about his victim.
ζ	*Trickery*	The villain attempts to deceive his victim.
θ	*Complicity*	The victim submits to deception, unwittingly helps his enemy.
A	*Villainy*	The villain causes harm or injury to a member of a family.
a	*Lack*	One member of a family lacks something or wants something.
B	*Mediation*	Misfortune is made known, hero is dispatched.
C	*Counteraction*	Seekers agree to decide on counteraction.
↑	*Departure*	The hero leaves home.
D	*1st function of donor*	Hero is tested, receives magical agent or helper.
E	*Hero's reaction*	Hero reacts to actions of the future donor.
F	*Receipt of magic agent*	Hero acquires the use of a magical agent.
G	*Spatial transference*	Hero led to object of search.
H	*Struggle*	Hero and villain join in direct combat.
J	*Branding*	Hero is branded.
I	*Victory*	Villain is defeated.
K	*Liquidation*	Initial misfortune or lack is liquidated.
↓	*Return*	The hero returns.
Pr	*Pursuit*	A chase: the hero is pursued.
Rs	*Rescue*	Rescue of hero from pursuit.
O	*Unrecognized arrival*	The hero, unrecognized, arrives home or in another country.
L	*Unfounded claims*	A false hero presents unfounded claims.
M	*Difficult task*	A difficult task is proposed to the hero.
N	*Solution*	The task is resolved.
Q	*Recognition*	The hero is recognized.
Ex	*Exposure*	The false hero or villain is exposed.
T	*Transfiguration*	The hero is given a new appearance.
U	*Punishment*	The villain is punished.

Figure 1.6. Propp's Functions   *(continued)*

W	Wedding	The hero is married and ascends the throne.
	There are seven dramatis personae in Propp's scheme and they are listed below and described:	
1.	Villain	Fights with hero.
2.	Donor	Provides hero with magical agent
3.	Helper	Aids hero in solving difficult tasks, etc.
4.	Princess and her father	Sought-for person Assigns difficult tasks
5.	Dispatcher	Sends hero on his mission.
6.	Hero	Searches for something or fights with villain
7.	False Hero	Claims to be hero but is unmasked

Figure 1.6. Continued

that is kept beneath the sea and is controlled by Number Two. Six is sent to the Village hospital, where he finds himself sharing a room with an old friend, also a spy. While Six is being examined by a doctor there is a commotion. Six rushes to his room and is told that the friend has committed suicide. After Six is released from the hospital he notices a woman acting strangely at the friend's burial procession. Six talks with the woman, who tells him she was the friend's lover and that they were planning to escape from the island. She has a watch with a special device that will enable Six to evade Rover and steal a helicopter. Six takes the watch and "escapes" via the helicopter, but shortly after he has left the island he discovers the helicopter is rigged and controlled by Number Two. The episode ends with the helicopter returning to the Village and the spy friend, who has supposedly committed suicide, telling Two that Six is an unusual person who will need special treatment.

Although *The Prisoner* is not a fairy tale, per se, it contains many elements of the fairy tale. Many contemporary narrative texts are, it can be argued, modified and updated fairy tales that, to a considerable degree, resemble the tales Propp described. Figure 1.7 lists a few of the Proppian functions that can be applied to events in "Arrival." This analysis could have been extended and made more detailed by citing some of the subcategories Propp (1968) uses in *Morphology of the Folk Tale,* but I only want to suggest the possibilities of this kind of analysis here.

There are several important things to be learned from a syntagmatic analysis. First, narratives, regardless of kind or genre, are composed of certain functions (or elements) that are essential for the creation of a story. Propp leads us, then, to understanding the nature of formulas.

Propp's Functions	Symbol	Events in "Arrival"
Initial situation	a	(implicit) spies can't resign
Interdiction violated	δ	hero abducted to the village
villain causes injury	A	hero abj\ducted to the Village
receipt of a magical agent	F	woman gives Six watch with device
false hero exposed	Ex	friend shown with Two

Figure 1.7 Proppian Functions in "Arrival" Episode of *The Prisoner*

Second, the order in which events take place in a narrative is of great importance. There is a logic to narrative texts and the arrangement of elements in a story greatly affects our perception of what anything "means." That, in fact, is what editing is.[2]

PARADIGMATIC ANALYSIS

The paradigmatic analysis of a text involves searching for a hidden pattern of oppositions that are buried in it and that generate meaning. As Alan Dundes writes in his introduction to Propp's *Morphology of the Folk Tale*, the paradigmatic form of structural analysis

> seeks to describe the pattern (usually based upon an a priori binary principle of opposition) which allegedly underlies the folkloristic text. This pattern is not the same as the sequential structure at all. Rather, the elements are taken out of the "given" order and are regrouped in one or more analytic schema. (Propp, 1968: xi)

There is a reason we search for binary or polar oppositions. It is because meaning is based upon establishing relationships, and the most important relationship in the production of meaning in language is that of opposition.

We return here to Saussure's (1966) notion that "in language there are only differences." Or, as Jonathan Culler has put it:

> Structuralists have generally followed Jakobson and taken the binary opposition as a fundamental operation of the human mind basic to the production of meaning. (1976: 15)

Thus in all texts (whether narrative or not) there must be some kind of a systematic and interrelated set of oppositions that can be elicited. Many people are not conscious of these polar oppositions—and sometimes

Freedom	Control
Number Six	Number Two
the individual	the organization
willpower	force
escape	entrapment
trust	deception

Figure 1.8 Polar Oppositions in "Arrival"

they are implied, and not given—but without differences there is no meaning.

Some people argue that the oppositions and other structures that semiologists "elicit" from texts are not really there. These critics assert that semiologists do not *discover* systems of relationships but, instead, *invent* them. This controversy is sometimes known as the "hocus-pocus" versus the "God's truth," problem. I believe that the bipolar oppositions that semiologists find in texts are actually there; not only that, but they *have* to be there. Finding meaning without discerning polar oppositions is like listening to the sound of one hand clapping.

Since I've used *The Prisoner* already, let me offer a paradigmatic analysis of "Arrival." The most important opposition found in this episode is between freedom and control and I use these two concepts at the head of my list of oppositions (Figure 1.8). This brief listing shows the ideational structure upon which the narrative is hung.

Claude Lévi-Strauss, the distinguished French anthropologist, suggests that the syntagmatic analysis of a text gives the text's manifest meaning and that the paradigmatic analysis of a text gives its latent meaning. The manifest structure involves what happens, and the latent structure involves what a text is about. Or, to put it another way, we are not so much concerned with what characters *do* as we are with what they *mean* when we use the paradigmatic approach.

What Lévi-Strauss is interested in is the way narratives are organized or structured and how their organization generates meaning. He has done a great deal of work (much of it highly controversial) on myths, kinship systems, and related matters. There are, he believes, fundamental or minimal units of myths, "mythemes," which combine in certain ways to give messages. These mythemes can be expressed in short sentences that express important relationships. For example, in the Oedipus myth, Lévi-Strauss offers mythemes such as "Oedipus kills his father, Laius" or "Oedipus marries his mother" or "Oedipus immolates the Sphinx." These mythemes and their rules of combination (what he calls "bundles" or relations) are the stuff of which myths are made. Myths are important because they not only function as charters for the groups that tell and believe them, but also because they are the keys to the ways in which the human mind works.

What is most significant about myths is the stories they tell, not their style. Thus the structured relationships among the characters and what these relationships ultimately mean should be the object of one's attention, not the way a story is told. Myths, Lévi-Strauss believes, give coded messages from cultures to individuals, and the task of the analyst is to discover these masked or hidden messages by "cracking the code," so to speak, in the final analysis this involves eliciting the paradigmatic structure of a text.[3]

In making a paradigmatic analysis of a text several errors should be avoided. First, make certain you elicit true oppositions (as opposed to mere negations). I would suggest that "poor" is the opposite of "rich" and should be used instead of something such as "unrich" or "nonrich." And second, be sure that your oppositions are tied to characters and events in the text.

If I had offered a more detailed synopsis of "Arrival" I would have been able to offer more detailed syntagmatic and paradigmatic analyses of this story, and my lists of Proppian functions and polar oppositions (Figures 1.7 and 1.8) would have been longer. I might add that it is useful to explicate the terms used in the list of oppositions and explain to the reader why each paired opposition is used.

INTERTEXTUALITY

Intertextuality is a term about which there is a good deal of controversy. For our purposes it will refer to the use in texts (consciously or unconsciously) of materials from other, previously created texts. Parody would be a good example of the conscious use of materials from a text. *A parody is a humorous imitation of a text.* In order for the parody to be effective, viewers must be familiar with the original text in order to appreciate the ways in which it is ridiculed in the parody. There can also be parodies of *style* (there are many contests which involve imitating Hemingway's style of writing) and *genre* parodies in which the basic plot structure of soap operas or westerns, or some other formulaic kind of text can be ridiculed. In some films, for example, directors create scenes which we can recognize as being "quotations" from other films. Avant garde film makers and other artists often consciously "quote" other artists—they patch together bits and pieces from well known works and create some kind of a new work.

Unconscious intertextuality involves the use of materials of one kind or another (such as plots, themes, or kinds of characters) that become common currency, that pervade cultures, and find their way, without anyone being aware of it, into texts. Some literary theorists argue, in fact, that all creative work is, ultimately, intertextual. That is, all texts are related to other texts, to varying degrees.

The Russian semiotician Mikhail Bakhtin has suggested that language is "dialogic," by which he means that when we speak, what we say is both tied to things that have been said before and to utterances that we expect to be made in the future. If we take this notion and move it from speech utterances to texts, we gain an insight into intertexuality. In a book of Bakhtin's essays, *The Dialogic Imagination,* he discusses the relationship that exists between texts. He writes, in his essay "From the prehistory of novelistic discourse" about what he calls the matter of "quotation" in the Middle Ages (which we now would call intertextuality):

> The role of the other's word was enormous at that time; there were quotations that were openly and reverently emphasized as such, or that were half-hidden, completely hidden, half-conscious, unconscious, correct, intentionally distorted, deliberately reinterpreted and so forth. The boundary lines between someone else's speech and one's own speech were flexible, ambiguous, often deliberately distorted and confused. Certain types of texts were constructed like mosaics out of the texts of others. . . . One of the best authorities on medieval parody . . . states outright that the history of medieval literature and its Latin literature in particular 'is the history of appropriation, re-working and imitation of someone else's property'—or as we would say, of another's language, another's style, another's word. (1981, 69)

What happened in the middle ages, the "appropriation" of the work of others, let me suggest, is similar to what happens today. And this is because, in part, we (in the western world, at least) share a common cultural heritage which informs our work and is reflected in texts even when there is not a conscious decision made to "quote" from other texts or sources.

METAPHOR AND METONYMY

Metaphor and metonymy are two important ways of transmitting meaning. In metaphor a relationship between two things is suggested through the use of *analogy.* Thus we might say, "My love is a red rose."

One of the most common metaphoric forms is the simile, in which "like" or "as" is used and a comparison is suggested. For example, we find similes in statements such as "He's as sharp as a razor," or "She's as good as an angel."

Sometimes we incorporate metaphors and similes in verbs we use. Consider the following examples:

The ship *cut* through the waves. (the ship is like a knife)
The ship *danced* through the waves. (the ship is like a dancer)
The ship *raced* through the waves. (the ship is like a race car)
The ship *pranced* through the waves. (the ship is like a horse)
The ship *plowed* through the waves. (the ship is like a plow)

In these examples, the ship takes on different identities. These verbs convey a different feeling from the statement "The ship sailed through the waves."

In metonymy a relationship is suggested that is based on *association,* which implies the existence of codes in people's minds that enable the proper connections to be made. As James Monaco writes in *How to Read a Film*:

> A metonymy is a figure of speech in which an associated detail or notion is used to invoke an idea or represent an object. Etymologically, the word means "substitute naming" (from the Greek meta, involving transfer, and onoma, name). Thus in literature we can speak of the king (and the idea of kingship) as "the crown." (1977: 135)

A common form of metonymy is a synecdoche, in which a part stands for the whole or vice versa.

A good example of metaphor in film is the famous scene in Chaplin's *The Gold Rush* in which he cooks his boots and eats the shoelaces the way one eats spaghetti. A good example of metonymy in *The Prisoner* would be the monstrous balloon, Rover, which symbolizes the oppressive regime that runs the Village. Figure 1.9 compares and contrasts metaphor and metonymy and should help to clarify the two concepts.

Generally speaking we find metaphor and metonymy all mixed together, and sometimes a given object might have both metaphoric and metonymic significance. The distinction is important because it enables us to see more clearly how objects and images (as well as language) generate meaning. And, in the case of metonymy, it becomes obvious that people carry *codes* around in their heads, highly complex patterns of associations that enable them to interpret metonymic communication

Metaphor	Metonymy
meta—transfer, beyond phor—to bear	meta—transfer onoma—name

Chaplin eats shoelaces like
  spaghetti
	Rover kills one of the villagers on
	  command of Number Two

simile: important subcategory
  in which comparison is made
  using "like" or "as
	synecdoche: important subcategory
	  in which part stands for the whole
	  or whole for a part

"No man is an island . . ."	red suggests passion
costume of Spiderman	Uncle Sam "stands for" America

long, thin objects can be seen
  as penises
	"bowler" implies Englishman;
	  cowboy hat implies the American West

Figure 1.9. Metaphor and Metonymy Contrasted

correctly. Just as you can't tell the players without a program, you can't understand the meaning of most things without knowing the codes.

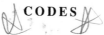 CODES

Codes are highly complex patterns of associations we all learn in a given society and culture. These codes, or "secret structures" in our minds, affect the way we interpret signs and symbols found in the media and the way we live. From this perspective, cultures are codification systems that play an important (though often unperceived) role in our lives. To be socialized and be given a culture means, in essence, to be taught a number of codes, most of which are quite specific to a person's social class, geographical location, ethnic group, and soon, though these subcodings may exist within a more general code, such as "American character," for example.

We all recognize that in order for one to be able to drive on the highways a code is needed. This code is a collection of rules that tells us what to do in all conceivable situations. In like manner, we are all taught (often informally) other codes that tell us what to do in various situations and, when we think of television, what certain things "mean." Quite obviously we carry over our rules and understandings about life to media productions or, as we now put it, "mass-mediated culture."

It is quite possible, then, for misunderstandings to arise between those who create television programs and those who view them. In his essay, "Towards a Semiotic Inquiry into the Television Message," Umberto Eco (1972: 106), the distinguished Italian semiologist, suggests that "the aberrant decoding . . . is the rule in the mass media." This is because people bring different codes to a given message and thus interpret it in different ways. As Eco puts it:

> Codes and subcodes are applied to the message [read "text" here] in the light of a general framework of cultural references, which constitutes the receiver's patrimony of knowledge: his ideological, ethical, religious standpoints, his psychological attitudes, his tastes, his value systems, etc. (1972: 115)

Eco offers some examples that suggest how these aberrant decodings might have taken place in the past: foreigners in strange cultures who do not know the codes or people who interpret messages in terms of their codes rather than the codes in which the messages were originally cast. This was, he tells us, before the development of mass media, when aberrant decodings were the exception, not the rule. With the development of mass media, however, the situation changed radically and aberrant decoding became the norm. According to Eco, this is because of the wide gap that exists between those who create and generate the material carried by the media and those who receive this material.

The transmitters of messages, because of their social class, educational level, political ideologies, world view, ethos, and so on, do not share the same codes as their audiences, who differ from the message transmitters in some or even most of the above respects and who interpret the messages they receive from their own perspectives.

The work of British sociolinguist Basil Bernstein illustrates how this might be possible. His research leads him to conclude that in Britain children learn either of two linguistic codes, the "elaborated" or "restrictive" codes, and that these codes play a major role in the children's future development and adult lives. The list below shows the differences between these two codes.

Elaborated Code	Restricted Code
middle classes	working classes
grammatically complex	grammatically simple
varied vocabulary	uniform vocabulary
complex sentence structure	short, repetitive sentences
careful use of adjectives and adverbs	little use of adjectives and adverbs
high-level conceptualization	low-level conceptualization
logical	emotional
use of qualifications	little use of qualifications
users aware of code	users unaware of code

These codes become the matrix through which thought is filtered, leading to very different value systems, belief systems, attitudes about the world, and so on. Bernstein's work enables us to see how language shapes us and demonstrates the enormous problems we face in trying to resocialize the hard-core poor and other disadvantaged elements in society.

It has been said that the United States and Great Britain are two nations separated by a common language. In the same manner, the different classes in Britain, with their different codes, seem to be separated. When you move from language to the media, where there are aesthetic codes, iconic codes, and more separating people, the fact that the media can communicate with any degree of effectiveness becomes quite remarkable.

There are a number of aspects of codes and questions related to them that I would like to mention (but not deal with in any detail here) and that anyone interested in codes would do well to consider and investigate:

Characteristics of codes: coherence, covertness, clarity, concreteness, continuity, comprehensiveness, and the like.

Manifestations of codes: personality (in psychology), social roles (in social psychology), institutions (in sociology), ideologies (in political science), rituals (in anthropology).

Problems: creation of codes, modification of codes, conflicting codes, countercodes, codes and rules.

Codes in popular culture: formulas in spy stories, detective stories, westerns, science fiction adventures, pop music, fanzines, girly fiction, horror stories, gothic novels, advertisements, sitcoms, and so on.

Ritual: meals, drinking in bars, gift giving, dating, watching television, supermarket shopping, behavior in elevators, sports contests, making love, dressing, and so on.[4]

Codes are difficult to see because of their characteristics—they are all-pervasive, specific, and clear-cut, which makes them almost invisible. They inform almost every aspect of our existence (I've listed some of their manifestations) and provide a useful concept for the analyst of the popular arts and media. For not only do genres such as the western or the sitcom follow codes, which are commonly known as formulas, but so do the media in general. It is to this subject I would like to turn now, specifically, with a discussion of codes in television.

SEMIOLOGY OF THE TELEVISION MEDIUM

I have, to this point, been concerned with the way in which semiological analysis can explicate programs carried on television, with a specific focus on the television narrative. A medium carries various genres of the popular arts, as the list below demonstrates:

Media	Popular Art Forms
radio	soap operas
television	advertisements/commercials
films	westerns
comics	police dramas
records	variety shows
posters	musicals
newspapers	talk shows
magazines	news
telephone	spy stories
books	documentaries
billboards	love stories

Each medium, because of its nature, imposes certain limitations on whichever popular art form or genre it carries. Because of the small screen and nature of the television image, for instance, it is difficult to do huge battle scenes. Television is a "close-up" medium better suited to revealing character than to capturing action.

In applying semiology to television, then, it makes sense to concern ourselves with aspects of the medium that *function as* "signs," as distinguished from carrying signs. What is most interesting about television, from this point of view, are the kinds of camera shots employed in the medium. The list below shows the more important kinds of shots, which function as signifiers, defines them, and suggests what is signified by each shot.

Signifier (shot)	Definition	Signified (meaning)
close-up	face only	intimacy
medium shot	most of body	personal relationship
long shot	setting and characters	context, scope, public distance
full shot	full body of person	social relationship

We can do the same for camera work and editing techniques:

Signifier	Definition	Signified (meaning)
pan down	camera looks down	power, authority
pan up	camera looks up	smallness, weakness
zoom in	camera moves in	observation, focus
fade in	image appears on blank screen	beginning
fade out	image screen goes blank	ending
cut	switch from one image to another	simultaneity, excitement
wipe	image wiped off screen	imposed conclusion

The above material represents a kind of grammar of television as far as shots, camera work, and editing techniques are concerned. We all learn the meanings of these phenomena as we watch television and they help us to understand what is going on in a given program.

There are other matters that might be considered here, also, such as lighting techniques, the use of color, sound effects, music, and so on. All of these are signifiers that help us interpret what we see on television (and also what we hear). Television is a highly complex medium that uses verbal language, visual images, and sound to generate impressions and ideas in people. It is the task of the television semiologist to determine, first, how this is possible and, second, how this is accomplished.

SOME CRITICISMS OF SEMIOLOGICAL ANALYSIS

You will notice that very little has been said up to this point about aesthetic judgments. This leads us to one of the major criticisms of semiological analysis, namely, that in its concern for the relationship of elements and production of meaning in a text, it ignores the quality of the work itself. That is, semiology is not really concerned with art, but rather with meaning and modes of cognition (the codes needed to understand a text). It is as if one judged a meal by the quality of the ingredients, without any concern for how the food was cooked or what it tasted like.

In certain cases, the text is subjugated by the critic. It exists as nothing but (or perhaps little more than) an excuse for a virtuoso performance by the semiologist, who grabs the spotlight away from the work itself. But this is a problem of all forms of interpretation. Most works of art exist now at the top of a huge mountain of criticism that analyzes and explicates them, sometimes at greater length than the original work itself.

Another problem with semiological analysis, especially of television and televised texts, is that we lack a strong theoretical foundation that would facilitate work in these areas. Most of the work done in semiology in recent years has concerned itself with film, not television. Without a strong and well-articulated body of theoretical criticism, work in the applied semiological analysis of television texts must remain tentative.

Nevertheless, a great deal is possible and, if we can avoid extremism in the analysis of signifying systems in our texts, we can produce critical readings of considerable value and utility. We have enough theory to get started, and applied semiological analyses are likely to lead to advances in critical theory.

A CHECKLIST FOR SEMIOLOGICAL ANALYSIS OF TELEVISION

In the material that follows I suggest some activities that should be undertaken in making a semiological analysis of a television program. I have concentrated on the narrative in this chapter, but much of what I've discussed is applicable to all kinds of programs.

(A) *Isolate and analyze the important signs in your text.*
    (1) What are the important signifiers and what do they signify?
    (2) What is the system that gives these signs meaning?
    (3) What codes can be found?
    (4) What ideological and sociological matters are involved?
(B *What is the paradigmatic structure of the text?*
    (1) What is the central opposition in the text?
    (2) What paired opposites fit under the various categories?
    (3) Do these oppositions have any psychological or social import?
(C) *What is the syntagmatic structure of the text?*
    (1) What functions from Propp can be applied to the text?
    (2) How does the sequential arrangement of elements affect meaning?
    (3) Are there formulaic aspects that have shaped the text?
(D) *How does the medium of television affect the text?*
    (1) What kinds of shots, camera angles, and editing techniques are used?
    (2) How are lighting, color, music, and sound used to give meaning to signs?

(E) *What contributions have theorists made that can be applied?*
  (1) What have semiological theorists written that can be adapted to television?
  (2) What have media theorists written that can be applied to semiological analysis?

I hope that the contents of this chapter will give you a sense of the semiological approach and enable you to apply this fascinating—and powerful—analytical tool. You can apply semiology to television, film, the comics, advertisements, architecture, medical diseases, artifacts, objects, formulas, conventions, organizations, friends, enemies, and just about anything in which communication is important—and in which there is signification.

NOTES

1. Peirce's system is called"semiotics" and differs somewhat from semiology, which has a linguistic base. But, for our purposes, we will consider them essentially the same.

2. For example, consider the difference order makes in the following two phrases, each of which contains the same words: "My husband was late . . ." and "My late husband was . . ."

3. Space does not permit me to dwell any longer on Lévi-Strauss. Readers interested in pursuing this subject are referred to the annotated bibliography that accompanies this chapter for works by and about Lévi-Strauss.

4. For an explication of these matters, see Berger (1976).

ANNOTATED BIBLIOGRAPHY

Bakhtin, M. M. *The Dialogic Imagination: Four Essays.* Edited by Michael Holquist. Translated by Caryl Emerson and Michael Holquist. University of Texas Press. 1981. Four essays by M. M. Bakhtin on literary theory, with a focus on the novel. After years of obscurity, Bakhtin has been "discovered" and his ideas have become extremely influential, especially his notion of dialogism, discussed in this book, and of "carnival," discussed in his book on Rabelais.

Barthes, Roland. *Mythologies.* Hill and Wang, 1972. A collection of short essays on everyday life topics, such as wrestling, soap powders, margarine, and steak and chips, and a long essay on semiological aspects of myth. A fascinating book and one of the most interesting examples of applied semiological analysis.

Barthes, Roland. *Writing Degree Zero and Elements of Semiology.* Beacon Press, 1970. Barthes deals with the basic concepts used in semiological analysis. He makes reference to some of the work he's done on food, fashion, furniture, and automobiles.

Berger, Arthur Asa. *Signs in Contemporary Culture: An Introduction to Semiotics.* Sheffield Publishers. 1990. An exploration of the basic concepts of semiotic theory along with applications of these concepts to various aspects of contemporary society. Each chapter contains both a discussion and application of a semiotic concept.

Berger, Arthur Asa. *Seeing is Believing: An Introduction to Visual Communication.* Mayfield Publishing Co. 1989. This book uses semiotic principles, along with others, to help readers become visually literate. It shows how we make sense of images and discusses photography, the visual media and related concerns.

Coward, Rosalind and John Ellis. *Language and Materialism: Developments in Semiology and the Theory of the Subject.* Routledge & Kegan Paul, 1977. An important theoretical work that deals with semiological thought and its relation to Marxism, the work of French post-Freudian Lacan, and other topics.

Culler, Jonathan. *Structuralist Poetics: Structuralism, Linguistics and the Study of Literature.* Cornell University Press, 1976. An excellent discussion of the basic principles of semiological analysis and application to literature. Another book by Culler, *Ferdinand de Saussure,* in the Penguin Modern Masters series, is also highly recommended.

Eco, Umberto. *A Theory of Semiotics.* Indiana University Press, 1976. Important theoretical analysis of semiotics that deals with its range of applications. An advanced text for readers with a good background in the subject. See also Eco's *The Role of the Reader.*

Fiske, John and John Hartley. *Reading television.* Methuen & Company, 1978. This is one of the most useful applications of semiological theory to television to be found. The authors devote a good deal of attention to codes and to specific texts.

Guiraud, Pierre. *Semiology.* Routledge & Kegan Paul, 1975. A very brief but interesting explication of semiological principles, originally published in the French "Que sais-je?" series. Focus is on functions of media, signification, and codes.

Leach, Edmund. *Claude Lévi-Strauss.* Viking Press, 1970. One of the more successful attempts to make Lévi-Strauss understandable to the general reader. Has some biographical material as well as chapters on myth, kinship, and symbolism.

Lévi-Strauss, Claude. *Structural Anthropology.* Doubleday & Co., 1967. A collection of essays on language, kinship, social organization, magic, religion, and art by the distinguished French anthropologist, an original mind and a great literary stylist.

Lotman, Yuri (Jurij). *Semiotics of Cinema.* Translated from the Russian by Mark E. Suino. Michigan Slavic Contributions. 1976. An application of semiotics to cinema which deals with narration, montage, plot, acting and other related topics. Lotman is identified with the Tartu school of Russian semiotics and applies its principles to art and culture. Another Lotman work, *The Structure of the Artistic Text,* has also been published by Michigan Slavic Contributions (located at the University of Michigan).

Propp, Vladimir. *Morphology of the Folktale.* University of Texas Press, 1973. A classic "formalist" analysis of fairy tales that has implications for the analysis of all kinds of other mass-mediated culture.

Saussure, Ferdinand de. *Course in General Linguistics.* McGraw-Hill, 1966. One of the central documents in semiological analysis and the source of many of the concepts used in the field.

Scholes, Robert. *Structuralism in Literature.* Yale University Press, 1974. An introduction to structuralist thinkers, with a focus on the analysis of literary texts but with obvious implications for other kinds of texts. The ideas of thinkers such as Jakobson, Lévi-Strauss, Jolles, Souriau, Propp, and Barthes are dealt with.

Sebeok, Thomas A. (ed.) *A Perfusion of Signs and Sight, Sound and Sense.* Indiana University Press, 1977 and 1978. Two important collections of applied semiological theory. Topics dealt with include clowns, medicine, faces, religion, nonsense, architecture, music, and culture.

Wright, Will. *Sixguns and Society: A Structural Study of the Western.* University of California Press, 1975. An ingenious application of the ideas of Lévi-Strauss, Propp, and others to the western.

2

MARXIST ANALYSIS

Marxist thought is one of the most powerful and suggestive ways available to the media analyst for analyzing society and its institutions. In this chapter we deal with such fundamental principles of Marxist analysis as alienation, materialism; false consciousness, class conflict, and hegemony—concepts that can be applied to media and that help us understand the ways media function. We pay particular attention to the role of advertising in creating consumer lust and offer some cautions about the danger of being doctrinaire.

Until a decade or so ago, there was rather little Marxist analysis in "mainstream" American literary and social thought. This is not to say that there were no Marxists, for this is not the case. It is just that the Marxists were always "voices crying in the wilderness," and not very many people took heed of these voices or took them seriously. This is beginning to change now, and we find an increasingly large number of Marxist historians, political scientists, economists, and critics.

The situation is complicated by the fact that there are a variety of kinds, or schools, of Marxism and Marxist thought seems to be changing rapidly. In the pages to follow I will offer a discussion of some of the more fundamental concepts of Marxism that can be applied to media and popular culture. Ironically, Marxism often seems to have more interesting things to say now about culture, consciousness, and related problems than it does about economics.

The discussion that follows leans heavily on the work of Erich Fromm, who argues that Marx was a humanist whose argument was essentially a moral one. I might point out, in passing, that many Marxists do not approve of the societies, created in his name but perverting his doctrine, found in the Soviet Union, Eastern Europe, Cuba, China, and elsewhere. That is, one can be a Marxist without being a Communist and without believing in the necessity of revolution and establishment of a classless society by violent means.

What follows is an outline of some of the most fundamental principles of Marxism—principles that I feel will be most useful for the media analyst. My plan is to provide a basic understanding of Marxism, so that the reader can apply Marxist concepts to the public art forms carried by the media. If you find that this kind of analysis offers valuable new perspectives and insights, you can pursue your study of the subject further with books listed and described in the annotated bibliography that accompanies this chapter. I will cite passages from a number of texts, that will be helpful, but, because of the limitations of space, they will form no more than an introduction to Marxist thought that can be used to make an applied Marxist analysis of media.

MATERIALISM

When we talk about Marxist thought being "materialistic," we are using the term in a special way—not as we traditionally use it in America, where "materialism" suggests a craving for money and the things that money can buy. For Marxists, materialism is more of a conception of history and the way society organizes itself. Let me start here with some quotations of crucial importance from Marx's *Preface to a Contribution to the Critique of Political Economy*.

First, his discussion of the relationship that exists between society and consciousness:

> In the social production which men carry on they enter into definite relations that are indispensable and independent of their will; these relations of production correspond to a definite state of development of their material powers of production. The totality of these relations of production constitutes the economic structure of society—the real foundation, on which legal and political superstructures arise and to which definite forms of social consciousness correspond. The mode of production of material life determines the general character of the social, political and spiritual processes of life. It is not the consciousness of men that determines their being, but, on the contrary, their social being determines their consciousness. (Marx, 1964: 51)

The mode of production, economic relationships, then, are the base or the "determinant elements" in our thoughts—though the relationship between our thoughts and society is a complicated one. This passage suggests that beneath the superficial randomness of things there is a kind of inner logic at work. Everything is shaped, ultimately, by the economic system of a society, which, in subtle ways, affects the ideas that men have, ideas that are instrumental in determining the kinds of arrangements they will make with one another, the institutions they will establish, and so on.

Marx also wrote in *The German Ideology:*

> The production of ideas, of conceptions, of consciousness, is at first directly interwoven with the material activity and the material intercourse of men, the language of real life. Conceiving, thinking, the mental intercourse of men, appear at this stage as the direct efflux from their material behavior. The same applies to mental production as expressed in the language of politics, laws, morality, religion, metaphysics of a people. Men are the producers of their conceptions, ideas, etc.—real, active men, as they are conditioned by the definite development of their productive forces and of the intercourse corresponding to these, up to its furthest forms. Consciousness can never be anything else than conscious existence. (1964: 74-75)

This passage is important because it brings people into the picture and suggests that though consciousness is socially produced, it always filters through the minds of real, live, active men and women and is not something that works automatically. There is always the possibility of men and women gaining an understanding of their situation and doing something about it. But more about this shortly. We have, now, our first important insight—namely, that "our" ideas are not entirely our own, that knowledge is social.

With all of the above in mind, there are some questions we might ask now:

(1) What social, political, and economic arrangements characterize the society whose media is being analyzed?

(2) Who owns, controls, and operates the media?

(3) What roles do the various media play in the society whose media productions are being dealt with? And what are the functions of the various popular art forms carried by the media?

(4) What ideas, values, notions, concepts, beliefs, and so on are spread by the media, and what ideas, values, and so on are neglected by the media? Why?

(5) How are writers, artists, actors, and other creative people affected by the patterns of ownership and control of the media?

THE BASE AND THE SUPERSTRUCTURE

In this section we begin to develop ideas found in the passages quoted earlier. What Marx described as the "base" represents the economic system found in a given society. This economic system, or mode of production, influences, in profound and complicated ways, the "superstructure," or institutions and values, of a given society. Here is a relevant quotation from Friederich Engels's "Socialism: Utopian and Scientific" on the matter:

> The new facts made imperative a new examination of all past history. Then it was seen that *all* past history, with the exception of its primitive stages, was the history of class struggles; that these warring classes of society are always the products of the modes of production and of exchange—in a word, of the *economic* conditions of their time; that the economic structure of society always furnishes the real basis, starting from which we can alone work out the ultimate explanation of the whole superstructure of juridical and political institutions as well as of the religious, philosophical, and other ideas of a given historical period. Hegel had freed history from metaphysics—he had made it dialectical; but his conception of history was essentially idealistic. But now idealism was driven from its last refuge, the philosophy of history; now a materialistic treatment of history was propounded, and a method found of explaining man's "knowing" by his "being" instead of, as heretofore, his "being" by his "knowing." (Tucker, 1972: 621)

What this passage offers is an understanding of how ideas are transmitted to man—through the institutions, philosophical systems, religious organizations, and arts found in a given society at a given time—that is, through the superstructure. Capitalism is not only an economic system but also something that affects attitudes, values, personality types, and culture in general.

How the base affects the superstructure is a problem that has caused a considerable amount of aggravation to Marxists. Economic relations may be the ultimately determining ones, but they are not the only ones, and it is a grave oversimplification to say that the superstructure is automatically shaped by the base and is nothing but a reflection of it—a position sometimes described as "vulgar Marxism." This point of view fails to recognize that an economic system is dynamic and always in a state of change—as is a given superstructure—and that people, leading real lives and capable of all kinds of actions, are involved also. In our discussion of superstructures we will focus on the public arts and media, institutions that many Marxists claim are crucial to the understanding of how consciousness is determined, shaped, and manipulated.

Let us look at what I've been talking about in diagrammatic form:

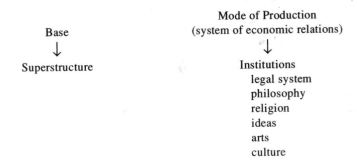

All of this might seem rather abstract and irrelevant until you recognize that the consciousness of people has important social, economic, and political implications.

FALSE CONSCIOUSNESS AND IDEOLOGY

The reason it is important to affect peoples' consciousness is that, by giving people certain ideas, it is possible for the wealthy, who benefit most from the social arrangements in a capitalist country, to maintain the status quo. Marx explained how the ruling class operates:

The ideas of the ruling class are, in every age, the ruling ideas: i.e., the class which is the dominant *material* force in society is at the same time its dominant *intellectual* force. The class which has the means of material production at its disposal, has control at the same time over the means of mental production, so that in consequence the ideas of those who lack the means of mental production are, in general, subject to it. The dominant ideas are nothing more than the ideal expression of the dominant material relationships, the dominant material relationships grasped as ideas, and thus of the relationships which make one class the ruling one; they are consequently the ideas of its dominance. The individuals composing the ruling class possess among other things consciousness, and therefore think. Insofar, therefore, as they rule as a class and determine the whole extent of an epoch, it is self-evident that they do this in their whole range and thus, among other things, rule also as thinkers, as producers of ideas, and regulate the production and distribution of the ideas of their age. Consequently their ideas are the ruling ideas of their age. (1964: 78)

According to this thesis, the ideas of a given age are those promulgated and popularized by the ruling class in its own interest. Generally speaking, then, the ideas people have are the ideas that the ruling class wants people to have.

The ruling class, we must recognize, believes its own messages. This is because it has within itself a group of conceptualizing ideologists who, as Marx put it, "make it their chief source of livelihood to develop and perfect the illusions of the class about itself" (1964: 79). By "ideology" I mean any system of logically coherent and widely applicable sociopolitical beliefs. The ruling class, according to this theory, propagates an ideology that justifies its status and makes it difficult for the ordinary people to recognize that they are being exploited and victimized.

This notion—that the masses of people are being manipulated and exploited by the ruling class—is one of the central arguments of modern Marxist cultural analysis. In a special issue of *College English* devoted to "Mass Culture, Political Consciousness and English Studies," Donald Lazere wrote:

Applied to any aspect of culture, Marxist method seeks to explicate the manifest and latent or coded reflections of modes of material production, ideological values, class relations and structures of social power—racial or sexual as well as politico-economic—or the state of consciousness of people in a precise historical or socio-economic situation. . . . The Marxist method, recently in varying degrees of combination with structuralism and semiology, has provided an incisive analytic tool for studying the political signification in every facet of contemporary culture, including popular entertainment in TV and films, music, mass circulation books, newspaper and magazine features, comics, fashion, tourism, sports and games, as well as such acculturating institutions as education, religion, the family and child-rearing, social and sexual relations between men and women—all the patterns of work, play, and other customs of everyday life. . . . The most frequent theme in Marxist cultural criticism is the way the prevalent mode of production and the ideology of the ruling class in any society dominate every phase of culture, and at present, the way capitalist production and ideology dominate American culture, along with that of the rest of the world that American business and culture have colonized. This domination is perpetuated both through overt propaganda in political rhetoric, news reporting, advertising and public relations, and through the often unconscious absorption of capitalistic values by creators and consumers in all the above aspects of the culture of everyday life. (1977: 755-766)

This passage suggests the all-encompassing nature of the Marxist approach and some of the most important objects of its attention. Quite obviously the media and popular culture are centrally important in the spread of false consciousness, in leading people to believe that "whatever is, is right."

From this perspective the mass media and popular culture constitute a crucial link between the institutions of society (and the superstructure in general) and individual consciousness.

The notion of manipulation has been attacked by German media theorist Hans Magnus Enzenberger as being useful but perhaps a bit dated:

> The New Left of the sixties has reduced the development of the media to a single concept—that of manipulation. This concept was originally extremely useful for heuristic purposes and has made possible a great many individual analytical investigations, but it now threatens to degenerate into a mere slogan which conceals more than it is able to illuminate, and therefore itself requires analysis. (1974: 100-101)

Enzenberger argues that the notion of manipulation is ultimately grounded on the assumption (the unspoken premise) that "there is such a thing as pure, unmanipulated truth," a notion he finds questionable, and one which is too limited. Ultimately, he argues, the left's antagonism to mass media benefits capitalism.

His hope is, perhaps, somewhat utopian. His notion is that all media manipulate; it is in the very nature of media:

> There is no such thing as unmanipulated writing, filming, or broadcasting. The question is therefore not whether the media are manipulated, but who manipulates them. A revolutionary plan should not require the manipulators to disappear; on the contrary, it must make everyone a manipulator. (Enzenberger, 1974: 104)

At this point we have moved away from analysis per se, and I will not pursue Enzenberger's thought any further. It may be that the theory of manipulation has deficiencies and drawbacks, but it still remains a central concept of Marxist media analysis for the simple reason that, as Marxists view society, the media are tools of manipulation. (The same argument about media manipulation can be used against socialist and Communist countries, though Marxist critics as a rule do not like to concern themselves with such matters.)

CLASS CONFLICT

For Marx, history is based on unending class conflict—unending, that is, until the establishment of a communist society, in which classes disappear and, with them, conflict.

The history of all hitherto existing society is the history of class struggles. Freeman and slave, patrician and plebeian, lord and serf, guild-master and journeyman, in a word oppressor and oppressed, stood in constant opposition to one another, carried on an uninterrupted, now hidden, now open fight, a fight that each time ended either in a revolutionary reconstitution of society at large, or in the common ruin of the contending classes. (Marx, 1964: 200)

The two classes that Marx talks about are the bourgeoisie, who own the factories and corporations and form the ruling class, and the proletariat, the huge mass of workers who are exploited by this ruling class and whose condition becomes increasingly more desperate.

The bourgeoisie, according to this theory, avert class conflict by indoctrinating the proletariat with "ruling-class ideas," such as the notion of "the self-made man" or the idea that the social and economic arrangements in a given society are "natural" and not "historical." If social arrangements are natural they cannot be modified, thus one must accept a given order as inevitable. Marxists argue that social and economic arrangements found in a given society at a given time are historical—created by people and therefore capable of being changed by people. The bourgeoisie try to convince everyone that capitalism is natural and therefore eternal, but this idea, say the Marxists, is patently false, and it is the duty of Marxist analysts to demonstrate this.

One of the approaches the ruling class uses is to convince people that there are no classes in a given society or that class is somehow incidental and irrelevant. Thus in America we have the myth of a "classless" society because we have not had a hereditary aristocracy and because our upper class tends to be friendly in social encounters. The president of a major corporation might call the doorman or janitor by his first name, but this, to the Marxists, is a means of camouflaging the real social relations that exist—though America, with its large middle class, does present special problems to Marxist analysts, since the likelihood of our having a revolution seems rather distant.

Nevertheless, the mass media still perform their job of distracting people from the realities of our society (poverty, racism, sexism, and so on) and of "clouding their minds" with ideas that the ruling class wishes them to have. In some cases we are offered heroes who reflect the bourgeois, ruling-class line and who reinforce and indoctrinate the masses who follow their activities in books, television programs, films, and so on. Generally speaking, the media serve either to mask class differences or to act as apologists for the ruling classes in an effort to avert class conflict and changes in the political order.

But the fact remains that for Marxists classes exist, and they are locked into hostile and mutually destructive relationships. As Marx wrote:

> Society as a whole is more and more splitting up into two great hostile camps, into two great classes directly facing each other—bourgeoisie and proletariat. (1964: 201)

The resolution of this dialectic is, for Marxists, inevitable, even though the media controlled by the ruling class or bourgeoisie may temporarily prevent the proletariat from attaining a true consciousness of its situation.

A French Marxist, Henri LeFebvre, has taken the concept of class conflict and manipulation and developed it into the notion that people living in capitalist societies are living in a state of "terror." In his book *Everyday Life in the Modern World* he explains this notion as follows. First, any society with radical class differences, with a small privileged class at the top and a mass of people living in poverty, has to be maintained by compulsion and persuasion. Second, these class stratified societies become over-repressive and develop sophisticated ways of masking repression and making unsuspecting individuals the instruments of their own repression and the repression of others. Finally, we arrive at the "terrorist" society in which:

> compulsion and the illusion of freedom converge; unacknowledged compulsions besiege the lives of communities (and of their individual members) and organize them according to a general strategy. . . . In a terrorist society terror is diffuse, violence is always latent, pressure is exerted from all sides on its members, who can only avoid it and shift its weight by a super-human effort; each member is a terrorist because he wants to be in power (if only briefly) . . . the 'system' . . . has a hold on every member separately and submits every member to the whole, that is, to a strategy, a hidden end, objectives unknown to all but those in power, and that no one questions. (1984: 147)

This notion, that people who live in capitalist societies are living in a state of terror, looks extreme, at first sight, but it may explain why there seems to be so much pressure on our lives and why many people feel so anxious about their lives and prospects.

LeFebvre wrote his book in 1968, when Marxism seemed to have answers for people and when the critiques it made of bourgeois societies seemed terribly telling. There was a sense of moral superiority that Marxists felt when they criticized class-ridden capitalist societies, full of exploited workers and impoverished people.

The events in the 1990s in Eastern Europe and the Soviet Union have shown that the Marxist-Leninist governments in these states only pretended to rule in the people's interest. They were class ridden and corrupt, and grossly inefficient as well. The rapid decline of communism as a viable form of government casts a dark shadow on LeFebvre's criticisms of capitalist societies. In reality, it could be argued that it was the communist societies that were terrorist, both overtly (in their use of military power and the secret police) and in terms of their impact on the psyches of their citizens.

And yet, it strikes me that LeFebvre does have a point and that his notion that people who live in bourgeois capitalist societies live in a state of psychological terror has some currency. In our everyday lives, we are under constant "attack" (by print advertisements, radio and television commercials, the programs carried by media) even though we may not recognize that we are being besieged or be able to articulate our feelings. (These terrors involve such matters as growing old in a youth-crazed culture, being fat in a thin-crazed culture, being poor in a wealth-obsessed culture, being a person of color in a white-dominated culture, being a woman in a male-dominated culture, and always being told or shown that we are suffering from deprivations, whether relative or absolute, and so on, endlessly.)

Whether these pressures we feel (if you don't want to use the term "terror") are primarily the result of living in complex modern, urban societies or of our specific social, economic and political arrangements is a question that has yet to be answered. For LeFebvre, the answer is clear.

ALIENATION

The word "alienation" suggests separation and distance; it contains within it the term "alien," a stranger in a society who has no connections with others, no ties, no "liens" of any sort. This notion is of central importance in understanding Marxism, which derives alienation from the capitalist economic system. Capitalism may be able to produce goods and materialist abundance for large numbers of people (though, ultimately, at the expense of others), but it necessarily generates alienation and all classes suffer from this, whether they recognize the fact or not.

There is a link between alienation and consciousness. People who live in a state of alienation (or condition of alienation) suffer from "false consciousness"—a consciousness that takes the form of the ideology that dominates their thinking. But, in addition to this false consciousness, alienation may be said to be unconscious, in that people do not recognize that they are, in fact, alienated. One reason for this may be that the alienation is so all-pervasive that it becomes invisible and hard to take hold of.

For Fromm and for many other interpreters of Marx, it is alienation that is the core of his theory. As Fromm writes in *Beyond the Chains of Illusion:*

> The concept of alienation has become increasingly the focus of the discussion of Marx's ideas in England, France, Germany and the U.S.A. . . . The majority of those involved in this debate . . . take a position that alienation and the task of overcoming it is the center of Marx's socialist humanism and the aim of socialism; furthermore that there is a complete continuity between the young and the mature Marx, in spite of changes in terminology and emphasis. (1962: 43-44)

This is a debatable position, Fromm adds. Whatever the case, the concept of alienation is very useful to analysts of popular culture.

The following quotations from Marx serve to illustrate his views on alienation:

> In what does this alienation of labour consist? First, that the work is *external* to the worker, that it is not a part of his nature, that consequently he does not fulfill himself in his work but denies himself, has a feeling of misery, not of wellbeing, does not develop freely a physical and mental energy, but is physically exhausted and mentally debased. The worker therefore feels himself at home only during his leisure, whereas at work he feels homeless. His work is not voluntary but imposed, *forced labour.* It is not the satisfaction of a need, but only a *means* for satisfying other needs. Its alien character is clearly shown by the fact that as soon as there is no physical or other compulsion it is avoided like the plague. Finally, the alienated character of work for the worker appears in the fact that it is not

his work but work for someone else, that in work he does not belong to himself but to another person. . . .

The *alienation* of the worker in his product means not only that his labour becomes an object, takes on its own existence, but that it exists outside him, independently, and alien to him, and that it stands opposed to him as an autonomous power. The life which he has given to the object sets itself against him as an alien and hostile force. (1964: 169-170)

Thus people become separated or "estranged" from their work, from friends, from themselves, and from life. A person's work, which is central to identity and sense of self, becomes separated from him or her and ends up, actually, as a destructive force. Workers experience themselves as objects, things that are acted upon, and not as subjects, active forces in the world. What people produce become "commodities," objects separated, somehow, from their labor. As people become increasingly more alienated, they become the prisoners of their alienated needs and end up, as Marx put it, "the *self-conscious* and *self-acting* commodity" (Fromm, 1962: 51).

In this situation the media play a crucial role. They provide momentary gratifications for the alienated spirit, they distract the alienated individual from his or her misery (and from consciousness of the objective facts of his or her situation) and, with the institution of advertising, they stimulate desire, leading people to work harder and harder. There is a kind of vicious cycle here: If, as Marx argued, work in capitalist societies alienates people, then the more people work, the more they become alienated. In order to find some means of escaping their alienation (which they do not recognize as a condition, but the symptoms of which they feel), they engage in various forms of consumption, all of which cost money, so that they are forced to work increasingly hard to escape from the effects of their work. Advertising has replaced the Puritan ethic in America as the chief means of motivating people to work hard; thus advertising must be seen as occupying a central role in advanced capitalist societies.

There is a debate among Marxist critics about the status of Franz Kafka, author of *The Trial* and *The Castle* and many other important works. His writings, critics suggest, show characters struggling with vast, anonymous bureaucracies and reflect the alienation that is so dominant in capitalist societies. The central question the critics argue about is whether Kafka suggested that alienation was a universal condition (and not just tied to capitalism).

Conservative Marxist critics attack Kafka for arguing that alienation is an inevitable condition of human beings and not recognizing that it could be overcome in Socialist countries. He did not understand, these critics argue, that alienation is historical, not natural and he did not suggest or show how alienation might be overcome—by setting up socialist societies (i.e., classless ones ruled by communists).

For liberal Marxist critics, Kafka showed that alienation can persist even in socialist countries (which are characterized by enormous bureaucracies) and he is valuable in pointing that out to everyone; he makes people aware of this alienation and this ultimately suggests that changes should be made and alienation can be eradicated. This critical debate, let me suggest, has been settled by history. The notion that only "socialist realism" is acceptable in art and literature is not taken seriously by many people, nor is "socialist realist" criticism.

THE CONSUMER SOCIETY

Advertising, as I have suggested, is an essential institution in advanced capitalist societies because it is necessary to motivate people to work hard so that they can accumulate money, which they can then use to buy things. But in addition people must be driven to consume, must be made crazy to consume, for it is consumption that maintains the economic system. Thus the alienation generated by a capitalist system is functional, for the anxieties and miseries generated by this system tend to be assuaged by impulsive consumption. As Marx wrote (about the effects of capitalism):

> Every man speculates upon creating a *new* need in another in order to force him to a new sacrifice, to place him in a new dependence, and to entice him into a new kind of pleasure and thereby into economic ruin. Everyone tries to establish over others an *alien* power in order to find there the satisfaction of his own egoistic need. (Fromm, 1962: 50)

Advertising generates anxieties, creates dissatisfactions, and, in general, feeds on the alienation present in capitalist societies to maintain the consumer culture.

There is nothing that advertising will not do, use, or co-opt in trying to achieve its goals, and if it has to debase sexuality, co-opt the women's rights movement, merchandise cancer (via cigarettes), seduce children, or terrorize the masses, all of these tactics and anything else will be attempted. One thing that advertising does is divert people's attention from social and political concerns into narcissistic and private concerns. Individual self-gratification becomes an obsession and, with this, alienation is strengthened and the sense of community weakened.

Thus advertising is more than a merchandising tool; advertising takes control of everyday life and dominates social relationships. And, at the same time advertising leads people to turn inward and to separate themselves from one another, it imposes upon them a collective form of taste. Advertising is a kind of popular art carried by the mass media, an art form that persuades and convinces and thus has an immediate (as well as a long-range) mission. The immediate mission is to sell goods; the long-range mission is to maintain the class system. In order to sell goods, advertising has to change attitudes, lifestyles, customs, habits, and preferences while at the same time maintaining the economic system that benefits from these changes.

A German Marxist, Wolfgang Fritz Haug, has developed a concept which is relevant here. Haug suggests that those who control the industries in capitalist societies have learned to fuse sexuality onto commodities and thus gain greater control of that aspect of people's lives that is of most interest to the ruling classes—the purchasing of goods and services.

In his book *Critique of Commodity Aesthetics: Appearance, Sexuality and Advertising in Capitalist Society,* Haug argues that the advertising industry, the servant of capitalist interests, has learned how to mould and exploit human sexuality, to alter human need and instinct structures. In his postscript to the eighth German edition of the book he writes:

> It would be particularly absurd in the case of commodity aesthetics to ignore the fact that its current dominant form is the aesthetics of the monopoly-commodity, i.e., the form in which transnational enterprises in particular intervene directly in the collective imagination of cultures. (1986: 11)

Thus, this power to use the appearance of products as a means of stimulating desire for them (the aesthetization of commodities) is now a worldwide phenomenon and people in many different countries are affected by it, as it "intervenes" in their cultures by capturing, so to speak, people's imaginations. People have the illusion that they make their own decisions about what to purchase and what to do. For Haug, to a remarkable degree, these decisions are made for people, whose acts turn out to be almost automatic responses to "stimuli" generated by advertising and the commodities themselves.

On the cover of Haug's book is a remarkable photograph. It shows pigeons in St. Mark's Square in Venice. The photo, taken from a height, shows that the pigeons form the name Coca-Cola. Workers scattered birdseed forming Coca-Cola and the birds flocked to the seed. As Haug explains:

> The pigeons did not gather with the intention of forming the trademark but to satisfy their hunger. But equally the seed was not scattered to feed the pigeons but employ them on its tracks as extras. The arrangement is totally alien and external to pigeons. While they are consuming their feed, capital is subsuming, and consuming, them. This picture, a triumph of capitalist advertising technique, symbolizes a fundamental aspect of capitalism. (1986: 118)

This photograph is most instructive. We (human beings living in societies dominated by capitalism and commodity aesthetics) are like the pigeons in the photograph; we fly to the things we want to consume under the illusion we are making individual choices and decisions while, in reality, we are being motivated by forces beyond our control and manipulated just like the pigeons.

In a later book, *Commodity Aesthetics, Ideology & Culture* (1987), Haug modifies his views. Haug argues in this book for a paradigm shift from what was essentially an economistic reading of Marx. This derived ideology, everyday life, and mass culture fairly directly from economic conditions. The new perspective focuses on the development of action "from below," and the capacity people have to resist domination and manipulation in the spheres of culture and economics, which are seen now as separate and distinct.

Nevertheless, the photograph of the pigeons strikes a chord. The photograph shows how our actions can seem motivated purely by personal desire and interest yet be, in reality, shaped and controlled by others, for their own purposes. The main instrument of this manipulation of people (as it was of the pigeons) is advertising and the mass media along with allied industries such as industrial design.

Marshall McLuhan's *The Mechanical Bride* analyzes advertisements (and comics) as cultural indicators and offers a number of brilliant insights into what specific advertisements reveal about American culture. In his chapter entitled "Love-Goddess Assembly Line," he compares Hollywood and advertising:

> So Hollywood is like the ad agencies in constantly striving to enter and control the unconscious minds of a vast public, not in order to understand it or to present these minds, as the serious novelist does, but in order to exploit them for profit. . . . The ad agencies and Hollywood, in their different ways, are always trying to get inside the public mind in order to impose their collective dreams on that inner stage. (McLuhan, 1967: 97)

The irony is that we are all convinced of our freedom to make our own choices since we believe our minds are "inviolable," while, in fact, our choices are ones that have been imposed upon us, in subtle ways, by the advertising industry. Our illusion of autonomy makes us all the more susceptible to manipulation and exploitation.

Advertising is part of what Hans Magnus Enzenberger (1974) has called "the consciousness industry" or "the mind industry." In his book, *The Consciousness Industry,* there is a chapter, "The Industrialization of the Mind," in which he writes about the ultimate selling job done by advertising and the media:

> The mind industry's main business and concern is not to sell its product: it is to "sell" the existing order, to perpetuate the prevailing pattern of man's domination by man, no matter who runs the society, and by what means. Its main task is to expand and train our consciousness—in order to exploit it. (Enzenberger, 1974: 10)

Advertising can be seen as an industry that uses radical methods for conservative reasons. There is, then, a special irony about the famous phrase used in the advertising industry, "Let's run it up the flagpole and see if anyone salutes." This is meant to be a testimony to advertising's pragmatism and openness to new ideas. What people are "saluting" when they do salute, however, is the old order.

BOURGEOIS HEROES

A great deal of media analysis involves dealing with heroic figures—men, women, animals, robots—who have a number of different functions in films, television dramas, comic books, commercials, and other dramatic forms. For some people heroes and heroines—and I am using the term in the sense of characters who are important (so that villains must also be considered) to dramas and other public art forms—reflect their age and society. For others heroes "shape" their age and help them transform their societies. In addition, heroes offer people models to imitate and thus help them to attain identities. At times these models are "deviant," so some heroes and heroines disturb whatever equilibrium society has obtained.

For Marxists, bourgeois heroes and heroines function so as to maintain the status quo by "peddling" capitalist ideology in disguised form and by helping keep consumer lust at a high pitch. One of the ideas bourgeois heroes sell is that of individualism, a value that takes many different forms (the self-made man, the American dream, the "me generation," and so on) but that always is connected to alienation, though few people see the connection. One of the early English Marxists, Christopher Caudwell, discusses heroes in his book *Studies in a Dying Culture*. In his chapter on T. E. Lawrence he writes:

> If any culture produced heroes, it should surely be bourgeois culture. For the hero is an outstanding individual and bourgeoisdom is the creed of individualism. . . . Indeed, bourgeois history, for bourgeois schools, is simply the struggles of heroes with their antagonists and difficulties. (Caudwell, 1971: 21)

This view of heroism, Caudwell feels, is naive, because it does not recognize that heroes are connected, intimately, to their societies and social and economic phenomena. He continues:

> What is it that constitutes heroism? Personality? No; men with the flattest and simplest personalities have become heroes. Is it courage? A man can do no more than risk and perhaps lose his life, and millions did that in the Great War. Is it success—the utilization of events to fulfill a purpose, something brilliant and dazzling in the execution, a kind of luring and forcing Fortune to obey one, as with that type of all heroes, Julius Caesar?

None of the above is adequate for heroism, for, as Caudwell sees it, heroism is independent of people's motives and is based on "the social significance" of people's acts. The heroes we tend to celebrate are what Caudwell calls "charlatans" who "have power over men but not over matter." Charlatans lack a societal reference and exist as alienated and alienating curiosities. "Society," writes Marx, "is not merely an aggregate of individuals; it is the sum of the relations in which these individuals stand to one another" (1964: 96). Thus the hero, for the Marxist, is the man or woman who understands this and who fights for a new social order—one in which the bourgeois values of individualism, consumer lust, and upper-class domination are smashed.

HEGEMONY

Hegemony is a concept that has been described by Raymond Williams (1977: 108; in *Marxism and Literature*) as "one of the major turning points in Marxist cultural theory." In its ordinary usage, "hegemony" means domination or rule by one state or nation over another. Marxists use the term in a different manner: Rule is based on overt power and, at times, on coercion, but hegemony is more subtle and more pervasive. As Williams (1977: 108) explains, rule is political and, in critical times, is based on coercion or force. Hegemony, on the other hand, is a complicated intermeshing of forces of a political, social, and cultural nature. Hegemony transcends (but also includes) two other concepts—culture, which is how we shape our lives, and ideology, which, from a Marxist perspective, expresses and is a projection of specific class interests.

Hegemony transcends culture as a concept because culture can be seen as being tied to "specific distributions of power and influence," or the mode of production and relations that stem from it. And hegemony transcends ideology as a concept because ideology is limited to systematized and formalized meanings that are more or less conscious. Ideology may be masked and camouflaged in films and television programs and other works carried by mass media, but the discerning Marxist can elicit these ideologies and point them out.

This is valuable, but only to a point, because ideological analysis does not cover enough territory, does not lead to the kind of profound analysis that hegemonial analysis makes possible.

Williams explains this as follows, saying about hegemony:

> It is distinct in its refusal to equate consciousness with the articulate formal system which can be and ordinarily is abstracted as "ideology." It of course does not exclude the articulate and formal meanings, values and beliefs which a dominant class develops and propagates. But it does not equate these with consciousness, or rather it does not reduce consciousness to them. Instead it sees the relations of dominance and subordination, in their forms as practical consciousness, as in effect a saturation of the whole process of living—not only of political and economic activity, nor only of manifest social activity, but of the whole substance of lived identities and relationships, to such a depth that the pressures and limits of what can ultimately be seen as a specific economic, political, and cultural system seem to most of us the pressures and limits of simple experience and common sense. Hegemony is then not only the articulate upper level of "ideology," nor are its forms of control only those ordinarily seen as "manipulation" or "indoctrination." It is a whole body of practices and expectations, over the whole of living: our senses, our assignments of energy, our shaping perceptions of ourselves and our world. It is a lived system of meanings and values—constitutive and constituting—which as they are experienced as practices appear as reciprocally confirming. It thus constitutes a sense of reality for most people in the society, a sense of the absolute because experienced reality beyond which it is very difficult for most members of the society to move, in most areas of their lives. (1977: 109-110)

for conclusion

Hegemony thus is what might be described as "that which goes without saying," or the givens or commonsense realities of the world, which, it turns out, serve an ultimate purpose—that of maintaining the dominance of the ruling class.

The works carried by the mass media can be seen, then, as not merely carriers of ideology that manipulate and indoctrinate people with certain views. The media, as unwitting instruments of hegemonial domination, have a much broader and deeper influence—they shape people's very idea of themselves and the world; they shape people's "world views."

Thus when using the concept of hegemony we must look very deeply into the work we are analyzing and elicit from it not only its ideological content but also its even more fundamental (and perhaps more insidious) ethological, worldview generating, content. We might think of hegemonial analysis as analogous to the work psychoanalysts do when they probe beneath symptoms to underlying root causes in the personality structure of patients. Williams say that hegemonial analysis is "cultural," but in a special sense, in that it connects culture to the patterns of subordination and domination that exist in a given society.

Let me offer another analogy that might be useful here. The concept of hegemony is similar to that of "paradigm" as used by philosophers of science. Paradigms refer to entire systems of thought that characterize historical periods and that play a major role in shaping the kind of science that we find in an era. Science shifts its paradigms every hundred years or so (or perhaps even less often), and with the paradigm shift, scientists see the world in new ways and work accordingly. The lists below aid in a comparison between "hegemony" and "paradigm":

law	popular arts
theory	ideology
paradigm	hegemony
SCIENCE	MEDIA ANALYSIS

In both cases the ultimate determinant of thought and behavior is not recognized, because it is so all-pervasive and fundamental. And just as the theory "explains" the law (or the event in nature that can be explained by law) so does the paradigm encompasses all the theories that are held. Likewise, the concept of hegemony encompasses all that exists in a society—ideological notions, works of popular art carried by the media, and so forth. And this makes analyses of media difficult, because it is hard to put one's finger on all the things we take for granted and assume are simply part of reality. We are, all too often, captives of the categories of bourgeois thought—the very thought we hope to expose as the instruments of our own domination.

THE DANGER OF BEING DOCTRINAIRE

Marxism, in general, and Marxist media analysis, in particular, have a great deal of appeal—especially to people with a strong sense of social justice and desires for a more egalitarian, more humane world. Despite the awesome complexity that Marxist thought often assumes, for Marxists the world becomes divided into two camps—the bourgeoisie, who own the instruments of production and are ultimately responsible for our alienation and a host of other ills from which we all suffer, and the proletariat and their allies, who want to save themselves and us. This is a great oversimplification, of course, but it also has a grain of truth; and in any flight between "good guys" and "bad guys," it is only natural to root for "the good guys."

In its best forms, Marxism is a humanistic system of thought that seeks to make it possible for people to have productive, useful lives. However, Marxism also is an ideology that explains everything (or nearly everything) in the world on the basis of certain axioms or beliefs from which everything else follows. And that is its danger.

The danger for the Marxist media analysts is that they know the answers *before* they ask the questions. That is, Marxists are also prisoners of the categories of their thought, and the questions they ask of a work of popular art carried by the media are often rather limited. Like the proverbial Frenchman who sees sex in everything (or the proverbial Freudian), the Marxist media analyst tends to see alienation, manipulation, and ideological exploitation in all of the public arts, and treats art of all kinds more in terms of its ideological content than anything else. This is terribly limited and does not do justice to a work of art.

What I am saying, then, is that there is a terrible danger of being doctrinaire and seeing works of popular culture (or anything else) *only* in terms of Marxist concepts and notions. This is not to say that there isn't an ideological dimension to much or most (or all, the Marxists would argue) of the material we deal with in analyzing media. There is and we must be mindful of it. But we must not neglect other aspects of a work—its psychological aspects, its moral aspects, its aesthetic components, and so on—and we shouldn't fit the material carried by media onto a Procrustean bed of Marxist notions.

There is also, of course, the possibility that Marx was wrong, and that his notions about the economic system's relation to culture are not correct or are too simplistic to be worth much. There is something destructive about a great deal of utopian idealism, and the fantasies that Marx dreamed of in his communist society may ultimately do a great deal of damage to people who do not recognize that the best is often the enemy of the good. Marx wrote:

> For as soon as the division of labor begins, each man has a particular, exclusive sphere of activity, which is forced upon him and from which he cannot escape. He is a hunter, a fisherman, a shepherd, or a critic, and must remain so if he does not want to lose his means of livelihood; whereas in communist society, where nobody has one exclusive sphere of activity, but each can become accomplished in any branch he wishes, production as a whole is regulated by society, thus making it possible for me to do one thing today and another tomorrow, to hunt in the morning, fish in the afternoon, rear cattle in the evening, criticize after dinner, in accordance with my inclination, without ever becoming hunter, fisherman, shepherd or critic. (1964: 97)

In the name of achieving this kind of society, however, most of the allegedly socialist Marxist states have set up repressive societies in which media is used for manipulation much more than it is in western bourgeois societies. If the Marxist media analysts are to be taken seriously as they point out the ways in which soap operas indoctrinate people into bourgeois values and mystify alienated housewives, this is an irony they must explain.

A NOTE ON MARXIST CRITICISM IN THE 1990s

In the first edition of this book, written in 1982, I suggested that Marxism seemed to have more interesting things to say about culture than about economics. I also pointed out that the Marxist societies that existed were highly repressive and that Marxist critics in the Western World did not see them as role models to which other countries might aspire.

Now, with the collapse of communism in Eastern Europe and the Soviet Union, the status of Marxism as a philosophy is being debated. If Marxism was the philosophy that informed (and was used to justify) repressive and totalitarian regimes—dominated all too often, it turns out, by ignorant sociopaths—how much credence can we put in it? Is Marxism dead, and if it is not dead, is it dying? At one time Marxists attacked Western capitalist societies in the name of a higher morality. Marxists argued that though they couldn't provide people the levels of material comfort found in Western societies, at least the Marxist regimes looked after people and did not exploit them. We now know that in most respects this was a sham.

I realized that Communism was dead years ago when I heard an interesting statistic: private farms occupied something like 3% of the land in the Soviet Union, yet provided something like 30% of the agricultural products. Marxism, to cut matters short, sounded good but simply didn't work. As the famous joke about work in Communist countries goes, "They pretend to pay us and we pretend to work."

What complicates matters is that there are many Marxisms and many different aspects to Marxist thought. As a political philosophy, it now lacks credibility, though there are still countries such as China where it is still the official philosophy. How long it will last in China remains to be seen. But as a means of criticizing culture, Marxism still seems to have some utility. You don't have to want to set up a society like the ones that existed in Romania or East Germany to be a Marxist, and Marxist culture criticism, to the extent that it points out the way media, and advertising in particular, help shape the consciousness of individuals and societies, still speaks to our moral sensibilities.

It is, I would suggest, the radical egalitarianism in Marxism that makes it appealing to people. Those who use Marxism, in its various incarnations and modernizations, as a tool of social criticism, do so in the name of freedom and quality. American Marxists, for the most part, want to establish a more democratic society here and see Marxism as the philosophy which provides the insights and concepts they need to make their criticisms of our society cogent.

Aaron Wildavsky, the distinguished political scientist, has suggested that in modern societies we find four political cultures: *hierarchical elitists, competitive individualists, egalitarians,* and *fatalists,* all of whom need each other. Hierarchical elitists believe in stratification and in the responsibility of those at the top to look after those below them. Competitive individualists are primarily interested in themselves, and want the freedom to compete fairly protected by the government. Egalitarians stress that people are equal in terms of their needs and that differences between people are social and not natural and should be played down. Fatalists believe in luck and opt out of the political system. They are all locked into complementary relationships, and all are necessary for the political order.

The egalitarians are critics of the hierarchical elitists and the competitive individualists (who form the backbone of democratic societies), and spend a great deal of time championing and trying to raise up the fatalists. It is this egalitarian sensibility which, I would suggest, motivates Marxist culture critics. Egalitarianism, as Seymour Martin Lipset pointed out in *The First New Nation,* is one of the core values of American society (along with achievement).

Whether Marxism is the best—or even a credible—philosophy to use as a means of analyzing and criticizing culture and the mass media is the question being debated now. Ironically, it may be that America will turn out to be the only place where Marxism is taken seriously.

Ultimately, each of us has to decide for himself or herself whether Marxism makes sense as a means of analyzing the media. If the concepts of the Marxists seem useful, seem to explain things better than other perspectives, use them. If not, find something else. Philosophies don't really die, I would argue. They are abandoned, and people turn their attention elsewhere. Whether Marxism will be abandoned and dumped on "the ash heap of history" remains to be seen.

ANNOTATED BIBLIOGRAPHY

Berlin, Isaiah. *Karl Marx: His Life and Environment.* Galaxy Books, 1963. A classic biography of Marx that also explains his ideas and their relation to his experiences.

Berger, Arthur Asa. *Agitpop: Political Culture and Communication Theory.* Transaction Books. 1990. A study of mass media and popular culture as they relate to political culture in the United States.

Caudwell, Christopher. *Studies and Further Studies in a Dying Culture.* Monthly Review Press, 1971. A remarkable stylist deals with literary figures, personalities, and concepts. His Marxism may be slightly "vulgar" or simplistic, but he has an incredible mind.

Enzenberger, Hans Magnus. *The Consciousness Industry: On Literature, Politics and the Media.* Continuum Books, 1974. An influential critic with some slightly unorthodox ideas.

Fischer, Ernst. *The Necessity of Art: A Marxist Approach.* Pelican Books, 1963. Sophisticated Marxist analysis of art, literature, and aesthetics, with interesting treatment of comics and other popular culture.

Fromm, Erich. *Beyond the Chains of Illusion: My Encounter with Marx and Freud.* Touchstone, 1971. A comparison of the ideas of Marx and Freud that serves as a useful introduction to the thought of both men.

Haug, Wolfgang Fritz. *Critique of Commodity Aesthetics: Appearance, Sexuality and Advertising in Capitalist Society.* 1989. University of Minnesota Press. A Marxist analysis of the role advertising plays in capitalist societies and the power design has to aestheticize objects and shape consumer behavior.

Lefebvre, Henri. *Everyday Life in the Modern World.* Transaction Books, 1984. A Marxist analysis of everyday life with important discussions of advertising, fashion, and terror.

Marx, Karl. *Selected Writings in Sociology and Social Psychology.* T. B. Bottomore and Maximilien Rubel, editors. McGraw-Hill, 1964. A collection of important passages from Marx's writings, organized and introduced by the editors.

Pappenheim, Fritz. *The Alienation of Modern Man*. Monthly Review Press, 1959. A wide-ranging study of alienation and its relation to philosophy, literature, technology, and politics, written from a Marxist perspective.

Rius. *Marx for Beginners*. Pantheon Books, 1979. A book of cartoons that explains the fundamental ideas of Marx and provides a dictionary of Marxist terms. Recommended for those who like books with lots of pictures.

Tucker, Robert C. (ed.) *The Marx-Engels Reader*. Norton, 1972. Almost 700 pages of Marx and Engels showing the evolution of their thought. Compiled by one of the foremost scholars of Marxism.

Williams, Raymond. *Marxism and Literature*. Oxford University Press, 1977. An influential British Marxist deals with culture and literature. The book has a useful bibliography of Marxist texts.

3

PSYCHOANALYTIC CRITICISM

Psychoanalysis is a therapeutic technique, but it is also a form of inquiry that has been applied to many areas—politics, anthropology, and literary criticism, to name a few. It yields interesting results, but results that are also generally controversial. In this chapter we explore the more significant aspects of psychoanalytic theory and show how the principles of psychoanalytic thought can be used to explain the hidden significance of cigarette lighters and *Hamlet,* among other things.

THE UNCONSCIOUS

Psychoanalytic criticism is a form of applied psychoanalysis, a science concerned with the "interaction of conscious and unconscious processes" and with the laws of mental functioning. It should not be confused with psychotherapy, which is concerned with treating mental illnesses and behavioral problems, though many psychotherapists use various kinds of analysis in their work. Instead it should be understood as one of many different forms of study that use psychoanalytic concepts to understand a particular subject matter. Thus there are psychoanalytically inclined sociologists, anthropologists, and political scientists, as well as critics, and all of them use concepts and insights from psychoanalytic theory in their work.

Freud did not discover the unconscious. Plato, Nietzsche, Bergson, and many others talked about it, but Freud did the most with it. And it is with Freud that all the neo-Freudians, post-Freudians, anti-Freudians, and non-Freudians must come to grips. He was a seminal thinker of incredible power and scope and his ideas and insights have fueled generations of scholars in numerous fields. What I will offer in this section is not a full-scale explication of Freudian thought, but a selection of some of his most important concepts—concepts that we can apply to the media that will help us understand how they work and how they affect us. Freud was most interested in helping people, but in the course of his amazing career he wrote on many other subjects, such as folklore, humor, and theatre—pointing the way toward the development of psychoanalytic criticism.

One of the keystones in psychoanalytic theory is that of the unconscious. As Freud writes in his essay "Psychoanalysis":

> It was a triumph for the interpretative art of psychoanalysis when it succeeded in demonstrating that certain common mental acts of normal people, for which no one had hitherto attempted to put forward a psychological explanation, were to be regarded in the same light as the symptoms of neurotics: that is to say they had a *meaning,* which was unknown to the subject but which could easily be discovered by analytic means. . . . A class of material was brought to light which is calculated better than any other to stimulate a belief in the existence of unconscious mental acts even in people to whom the hypothesis of something at once mental and unconscious seems strange and even absurd. (1963: 235-236)

We are not, then, aware of everything that is going on in our minds. Not only that, we are aware of only a little that is going on in our minds; only a small portion of our mental life is accessible to us.

It is frequently suggested that our mental life can be represented by an iceberg. The tip of the iceberg that we see above the water is what we are conscious of. The remainder of the iceberg, and by far the greater part of it, lies buried beneath the water. Though it is not seen, it is still there. "What is in your mind," Freud wrote in "One of the Difficulties of Psychoanalysis," "is not identical with what you are conscious of; whether something is going on in your mind and whether you hear of it, are two different things" (Freud, 1963: 189).

This means we are not in complete control of ourselves all the time, we are affected in ways we cannot fathom, and we do things for reasons we do not understand or will not admit to ourselves. In short, we are not completely rational creatures who act only on the basis of logic and intelligence, but instead are vulnerable to emotional and other kinds of nonrational or irrational appeals.

But why, you may ask, don't we become conscious of all that is going on in our minds? Why does all this material elude us? Why do our minds play such tricks on us? Freud offered an explanation that is both obvious (once it is pointed out) and ingenious: We *repress* this material because we do not want, for a variety of reasons, to become conscious of it. It would cause us pain or guilt or some other unpleasant feeling. Thus we create a barrier between our consciousness and our unconscious and do not allow repressed material through it.

Ernest Dichter is one of the founding fathers of the field known as motivation research. The goal of motivation research is to discover the unconscious and, it is assumed, the real reasons that people do things so that manufacturers and others can better shape people's behavior—that is, get them to buy their products or do whatever it is that is asked of them. In *The Strategy of Desire*, Dichter wrote:

> Whatever your attitude toward modern psychology or psychoanalysis, it has been proved beyond any doubt that many of our daily decisions are governed by motivations over which we have no control and of which we are often quite unaware. (1960: 12)

Dichter and other motivation researchers, then, "mine" the unconscious and put it to work, so to speak.

Dichter offers us an example of the way in which unconscious desires and forces operate in his discussion of cigarette lighters:

> The reliability of a lighter is important because it is integrally connected with the basic [read "unconscious" here] reason for using a lighter. (1964: 341)

Let me interrupt here to ask what you think this "basic reason" might be. The answer most people would give would be, "That's obvious—to light cigarettes." But that is the conscious, or "manifest," reason. The basic, or "real," reason, the "latent" and unconscious reason is something entirely different.

Let us return to Dichter, who tells us why people use lighters:

> The basic reason for using a lighter [is]—the desire for mastery and power. The capacity to summon fire inevitably gives every human being, child or grownup, a sense of power. Reasons go far back into man's history. Fire and the ability to command it are prized because they are associated not only with warmth, but also with life itself. As attested to by the Greek

legend of Prometheus and many other myths, the ability to control fire is an age-old symbol of man's conquest of the physical world he inhabits.

A cigarette lighter provides conspicuous evidence of this ability to summon fire. The ease and speed with which the lighter works enhances the feeling of power. The failure of a lighter to work does not just create superficial social embarrassment, it frustrates a deep-seated desire for a feeling of mastery and control. (1964: 341)

Thus cigarette lighters are important to people because they take care of powerful but unconscious strivings and needs they have. The same can be said of many of the films we see, television programs we watch, novels we read, and other art forms we find so necessary to our lives. That is because all of these things feed our unconscious lives, our psyches, in ways that few people understand.

But this need for mastery and power is only part of the story, for at a deeper level there is something else that is connected with our humble cigarette lighters. Dichter explains this as follows:

Research evidence suggests that at a still deeper level the need for certainty that a cigarette lighter will work matters as much as it does because it is also bound up with the idea of sexual potency. The working of the lighter becomes a kind of symbol of the flame which must be lit in consummating sexual union. (1964: 341)

This leads us to our next important subject—sexuality. Many people know that Freud was interested in sexuality, but know little more than that. And what they do know about Freud's views are usually simplistic, erratic, and absurd.

SEXUALITY

Freud's view of sexuality has caused many people to see him in negative and even hostile ways. This is because, I suggest, many people have mistaken notions of what he believed and also because we all tend to be extremely sensitive about this area. We all *resist*, then, intrusions into these most private and personal aspects of our lives and we may even repress—refuse to admit to consciousness—ideas and insights that would explain sexuality in general and our behavior in particular.

Freud described the "force by which the sexual instinct is represented in the mind" as the *libido*. It should be understood broadly and not as being restricted to sexual relations. That is, *libido* refers to various kinds of sensual pleasures and gratifications we can obtain. According to

Freud, every individual passes through four stages in his or her development: the *oral*, the *anal*, the *phallic*, and the *genital*. In *The Encyclopedia of Psychoanalysis* the stages are described:

> The mouth represents an erotogenic zone for the infant. Sucking and later eating represent the gratification of oral needs. The fact that the infant often sucks a pacifier indicates that he is not only concerned with the incorporation of calories. When the infant begins to have teeth, the need to bite expresses his sadistic desires. The second stage of development is usually referred to as the sadistic-anal, and is characterized by the infant's interest in excreting or retaining his stools. Finally, the third stage is referred to as the phallic, in which the boy is interested in his penis and the girl in her clitoris. The boy's interest in his penis appears to be responsible for his positive Oedipus complex, which is finally dissolved by the fear of castration. The girl reacts with penis envy, if she considers her clitoris to be an inferior organ to the penis.

> Freud pointed out that the stages are not clear-cut, and that the fourth stage, the genital phase, is achieved only with puberty. (Eidelberg, 1968: 210-211)

During infancy and childhood, our sexual life is rich, but dissociated and unfocused. This focusing occurs at puberty.

One of the difficulties in explaining psychoanalytical theory is that you seem to have to know everything at the same time. In the above quotation there were a number of concepts mentioned that might need a bit of amplification. For instance, there is the matter of *anality*; the *Oedipus complex* also requires more explication; and there are also the related concepts of *castration anxiety* and *penis envy*. These concepts are difficult for many people to accept and strike those not familiar with Freud and psychoanalytic thought as fantastic and farfetched. Perhaps it is best to think of all of the above-named as concepts developed by Freud to explain phenomena and behavior he encountered. Freud described psychoanalysis as "always incomplete and always ready to correct or modify its theories" (1963: 251).

Let us start with the matter of anal behavior, or what Freud called "anal eroticism," in a fascinating paper entitled "Character and Anal Eroticism." Freud connects a combination of personality traits that have developed to an extreme degree—orderliness, parsimoniousness, and obstinacy—with people who have had problems overcoming their anal stage, and who may use these personality traits as a means of dealing with it. What is most fascinating is that there are "connections which exist between the two complexes of interest in money and of defecation,

which seem so dissimilar" that are, or appear to be, "most far-reaching."
He writes:

> In reality, wherever archaic modes of thought predominate or have per-
> sisted—in ancient civilizations, in myth, fairy-tale and superstition, in
> unconscious thoughts and dreams, and in the neuroses—money comes into
> the closest relation with excrement. We know how the money which the
> devil gives his paramours turns to excrement after his departure, and the
> devil is most certainly nothing more than a personification of the uncon-
> scious instinctual forces. (Freud, 1963: 31)

Ultimately there is an identification of gold with feces, "the most
precious substance known to man and the most worthless" (Freud,
1963: 32).

THE OEDIPUS COMPLEX

The Oedipus complex represents the core of neurosis for Freud, and
is a concept that explains a great deal. In a famous letter written October
15, 1897 to Wilhelm Fliess, Freud describes how he came to recognize
the existence and importance of the Oedipus complex:

> Being entirely honest with oneself is a good exercise. Only one idea of
> general value has occurred to me. I have found love of the mother and
> jealousy of the father in my own case too, and now believe it to be a general
> phenomena of early childhood, even if it does not always occur so early as
> in children who have been made hysterics. . . . If that is the case, the
> gripping power of *Oedipus Rex,* in spite of all the rational objections to the
> inexorable fate that the story presupposes, becomes intelligible, and one
> can understand why later fate dramas were such failures. Our feelings rise
> against any arbitrary individual fate . . . but the Greek myth seizes on a
> compulsion which everyone recognizes because he has felt traces of it in
> himself. Every member of the audience was once a budding Oedipus in
> fantasy, and this dream-fulfillment played out in reality causes everyone
> to recoil in horror, with the full measure of repression which separates his
> infantile from his present state.
>
> The idea has passed through my head that the same thing may lie at the
> root of *Hamlet.* I am not thinking of Shakespeare's conscious intentions,
> but supposing rather that he was impelled to write it by a real event because
> his own unconscious understood that of his hero. How can one explain the
> hysteric Hamlet's phrase "So conscience doth make cowards of us all," and
> his hesitation to avenge his father by killing his uncle, when he himself so

casually sends his courtiers to their death and despatches Laertes so quickly? How better than by the torment roused in him by the obscure memory that he himself had meditated the same deed against his father because of passion for his mother—"use every man after his desert, and who should scape whipping?" His conscience is his unconscious feeling of guilt. (Grotjahn, 1966: 84-85)

According to psychoanalytic theory we all pass through a stage in which we desire our parent of the opposite sex—all of this, of course, on an unconscious level. Most individuals learn to master their Oedipus complexes; neurotic individuals are plagued by them. In little boys this mastery is aided by an unconscious fear of castration that takes hold of them—castration anxiety—and in little girls by jealousy of men and what is termed "penis envy."

Little boys, according to Freudian theory, sexualize their love for their mothers and wish to displace their fathers and monopolize their mothers' affection. Their fear of retaliation by their fathers leads them to renounce their love of their mothers, to identify with the masculinity of their fathers, to rechannel their love outside of the family and to direct their interest toward other females.

With little girls, the situation is different. They do not have to fear castration (some theorists suggest they believe they have already lost their penises), and do not relinquish their Oedipal desires as quickly as boys do. It lingers on much longer. But the girls do fear loss of love by their parents. Girls avoid this loss by re-identifying with their mothers and turning, eventually, to other males as a means of obtaining babies (and indirectly their lost penises).

There are several other related complexes that are of interest. There is, for example, the "Heracles complex" that is characterized by a hatred of the father for his children. Here, things are reversed and the father wishes to get rid of the children, who are seen as rivals for the affection of the wife. And there is the "Jocasta complex" (she was the mother of Oedipus) that has varying degrees of intensity. It varies from an over attachment by the mother to her son to incestual relationships.

One of the ways young children deal with their Oedipal anxieties is by listening to fairy tales. In *The Uses of Enchantment*, Bruno Bettelheim devotes a chapter to "Oedipal Conflicts and Resolutions" and argues that fairy tales help boys and girls resolve their problems through these stories. Children identify with the heroes and heroines of these stories and learn important things about life, as well.

The stories, Bettelheim suggests, speak to the children indirectly and symbolically—the stories are often about some unlikely hero who "proves himself by slaying dragons, solving riddles, and living by his wits and goodness until eventually he frees the beautiful princess, marries her, and lives happily ever after" (1977: 111). In stories that speak to little girls, there is usually some evil stepmother or enchantress who is intensely jealous and tries to prevent some hero, such as Prince Charming, from finding his princess. Sometimes in these tales the mother is split into two characters—an evil stepmother and a good mother (or fairy godmother).

Fairy tales are important for children because they help the children cope with the psychological difficulties they experience. As Bettelheim explains:

> Through the centuries (if not millennia) during which, in their retelling, fairy tales became ever more refined, they came to convey at the same time overt and covert meanings—came to speak simultaneously to all levels of the human personality, communicating in a manner which reaches the uneducated mind of the child as well as that of the sophisticated adult. Applying the psychoanalytic model of the human personality, fairy tales carry important messages to the conscious, preconscious and unconscious mind, on whatever level each is functioning at the time. By dealing with universal human problems, particularly those which preoccupy the child's mind, these stories speak to his budding ego and encourage its development, while at the same time relieving preconscious and unconscious pressures. As the stories unfold, they give conscious credence and body to id pressures and show ways to satisfy these that are in line with ego and superego requirements. (1977: 5, 6)

Fairy tales, and other texts which are very much like (they may be, in truth, modernized) fairy tales, have important functions as far as our psyches are concerned.

I cannot resist pointing out, in passing, that in *Star Wars,* the relationship between Luke Skywalker and Darth Vader is (we discover later) an Oedipal one. *Star Wars* is, to a great degree, a modernized fairy tale about a princess in distress and a young man who rescues her. There are other elements in the film as well—Germanic villains and World War II airplane battles, but the core of the film is, I would suggest, a fairy tale.

We must keep in mind that all of these phenomena operate beyond our consciousness and are kept buried through our power to resist and repress things that would disturb us. We empathize with Hamlet and with countless other heroes and heroines because, unconsciously, we recognize that their battles are our battles and their difficulties are our difficulties.

ID, EGO, AND SUPEREGO

The id, ego, and superego are part of what is usually referred to as Freud's "structural" hypothesis about mental functioning. In *An Elementary Textbook of Psychoanalysis,* Charles Brenner offers the following brief description of these three phenomena:

> We may say that id comprises the psychic representatives of the drives, the ego consists of those functions which have to do with the individual's relation to his environment, and the superego comprises the moral precepts of our minds as well as our ideal aspirations.
>
> The drives, of course, we assume to be present from birth, but the same is certainly not true of interest in or control of the environment on the one hand, nor of any moral sense or aspirations on the other. It is obvious that neither of the latter, that is neither the ego nor the superego develops till sometime after birth.
>
> Freud expressed this fact by assuming that the id comprised the entire psychic apparatus at birth, and that the ego and superego were originally parts of the id which differentiated sufficiently in the course of growth to warrant their being considered as separate functional entities. (1974: 38)

Each of these entities, the id, ego, and superego, are in themselves extremely complicated, and Freud and others have written a great deal about how they develop, how they function, and their importance to our psychic life.

The structural hypothesis superseded Freud's earlier theory of mental functioning, known as the "topographic," which divided the psyche into three systems: conscious, preconscious, and unconscious. I have dealt with these notions already, though I left out the preconscious in order to simplify matters. In essence the structural hypothesis sees the psyche in constant warfare, as the id and superego war against one another. In this war the poor ego tries to mediate between our desires for pleasure and our fear of punishment, between our drives and our consciences.

Freud's description of the id in his *New Introductory Lectures on Psychoanalysis* is most graphic:

> We can come nearer to the id with images, and call it chaos, a cauldron of seething excitement. We suppose that it is somewhere in direct contact with somatic processes, and takes over from them instinctual needs and gives them mental expression, but we cannot say in what substratum this contact is made. These instincts fill it with energy, but it has no organization and no unified will, only an impulsion to obtain satisfaction for the instinctual

needs, in accordance with the pleasure-principle. (quoted in Hinsie and Campbell, 1970: 372)

This bubbling cauldron of sexual desire, passion, lust, desire—what you will—must not be allowed to determine our actions since we live in societies and civilization demands that we control our behavior. The demands that civilization makes are so great, as a matter of fact, that we suffer from great psychological pain. (This is discussed in Freud's [1962] *Civilization and Its Discontents*.)

The superego corresponds, Brenner says, "in a general way to what we ordinarily call conscience. It comprises the moral functions of the personality." He lists the functions of the superego:

> 1. the approval or disapproval of actions and wishes on the grounds of rectitude. 2. critical self-observation. 3. self-punishment. 4. the demand for reparation or repentance of wrong-doing. 5. self-praise or self-love as a reward for virtuous or desirable thoughts and actions. Contrary to the ordinary meaning of "conscience," however, we understand that the functions of the superego are often largely or completely unconscious. (Brenner, 1974: 111-112)

The superego assumes, then, a position in opposition to the id. In between these two polarities the ego tries to mediate and operate with the aim, always, of self-preservation. It does this by storing up experiences in the memory, avoiding excessively strong stimuli by flight, adapting to moderately strong stimuli, and bringing about changes in the world by activity.

We can use these concepts to help understand texts. In certain texts, characters may be seen as primarily id figures or ego figures or superego figures. For example, in *Star Trek,* I would suggest that Spock is, essentially, an ego figure, Kirk (in German, interestingly, the name means "church") is a super-ego figure, and McCoy is an id figure. Spock, the emotionless Vulcan, represents pure rationality. Kirk, the commander of the Enterprise, more or less determines what it is to be done, and represents the super-ego. And McCoy, who is very emotional and operates, generally, on the basis of his feelings, represents the id.

In some texts, it is easy to identify a character as an id, ego, or super-ego figure. Superman, Dick Tracy, Luke Skywalker, and countless other heroes and heroines, and caped crusaders are obviously super-ego figures. But other heroes and heroines, such as James Bond or Indiana Jones, are more complicated and are more id and ego figures, perhaps, than super-ego ones. Villains, of course, are almost always id figures; they lack super-ego development and are only interested in gratifying their desires. They may be intelligent and shrewd, but they lack a sense of right and wrong.

We can also look upon genres in terms of the Freudian structural hypothesis. Certain kinds of films and television programs, such as news shows, interviews, and documentaries can be classified as essentially ego texts. Other texts, such as those featuring the police or, for example, religious television shows, are obviously super-ego texts. And finally, soap-operas and television programs and films involving sexuality (video pornography, MTV) tend to be id texts. It is not always possible to label a text as one or the other but in some cases, especially when we are dealing with formulaic works, it does make sense.

SYMBOLS

Psychoanalysis is, remember, an interpretative art. It seeks to find meaning in the behavior of people and in the arts they create. One way we can apply psychoanalytic theory is by understanding how the psyche works and learning how to interpret the hidden significance of what people and characters in fictions do. We ask ourselves questions, such as, "What does it mean when Hamlet says this or that?" or "What does it mean when Hamlet is unable to act?" We want to know *why*.

This is where symbols come in. Symbols are things that stand for other things, many of which are hidden or, at least, not obvious. A symbol can stand for an institution, a mode of thought, an idea, a wish—any number of things. Heroes and heroines are often symbolic and can be interpreted, then, in terms of all the things they stand for. And much of what is most interesting about symbols is their relation to the unconscious. Symbols are keys that enable us to unlock the doors shielding our unconscious feelings and beliefs from scrutiny. Symbols are messages from our unconscious.

Hinsie and Campbell define symbolism as follows:

> The act or process of representing an order or idea by a substitute object, sign, or signal. In psychiatry, symbolism is of particular importance since it can serve as a defense mechanism of the ego, as where unconscious (and forbidden) aggressive or sexual impulses come to expression through symbolic representation and thus are able to avoid censorship. (1970: 734)

According to this theory, then, we mask our unconscious sexual and aggressive desires by symbolization, which enables us to escape guilt from the superego.

There are a number of difficulties we face in interpreting symbols. (I might point out that there are a number of different theories in psychology about symbols and they have, like many other aspects of psychoanalytic thought, generated a great deal of controversy.) First, symbols are often ambivalent and can be explained in varying ways depending upon one's orientation. For some people Hamlet's inability to act symbolizes the power of an unresolved Oedipus complex, while for others it symbolizes his skepticism and overintellectualism. Some think Hamlet was paralyzed by grief and others think he was insane. If you are interested in the "problem" of Hamlet you should read *Hamlet and Oedipus* by Ernest Jones, for a fascinating, though doctrinaire Freudian, interpretation of this symbolic hero.

Symbols are also classified as conventional, accidental, and universal. *Conventional* symbols are words we learn that stand for things. In contrast to them we find *accidental* symbols, which are personal, private, and connected to someone's life history. A person may have fallen in love for the first time in Paris, so Paris may be his or her accidental symbol for love. (The accidental symbols we find in dreams are what make interpreting dreams so complicated a task, though dreams contain more than accidental symbols.) Finally, there are *universal* symbols, in which the relationship between the symbol and what is symbolized is intrinsic, or rooted in the experience of all people. Many of these are connected to our bodies and to natural processes. What makes matters particularly complicated is the fact that the logic behind symbolization is not the same logic we use in our everyday reasoning processes.

A comparison can be made between dreams and mass-media productions. For a long time neither were considered important, neither were thought to have any effects upon us, and neither attracted much serious attention. Now we know better. Dreams tend to be visual, so they are best compared with media such as film, television, and the comics. And just as dreams can be interpreted, by analyzing their symbolic content, so can mediated dreams such as we find in the cinema or on the television screen. In both cases we ask the same questions: What is going on? What disguises are there? What gratifications do we get? What do the various symbolic heroes and heroines tell us about ourselves and our societies?

DEFENSE MECHANISMS

Defense mechanisms are various techniques employed by the ego to control instincts and ward off anxieties. All of us make use of the various mechanisms at one time or another, though we are seldom conscious of doing so. In like manner, much of what the media brings us involves human beings in varying kinds of relationships, so many of the characters we see or read about can be interpreted (often) in terms of the defense mechanisms. That is, their behavior makes more sense to us when we can relate it to the defenses people use to maintain their equilibrium. In like manner we can also understand our fascination with media in terms of defense mechanisms.

What follows is a listing of the more important defense mechanisms, with a brief description of each.

Ambivalence: a simultaneous feeling of love and hate or attraction and repulsion toward the same person or object. Sometimes these feelings alternate in rapid succession in people who wish to be able to gratify contradictory wishes.

Avoidance: a refusal to become involved with subjects that are distressing because they are connected to unconscious sexual or aggressive impulses.

Denial or disavowal: a refusal to accept the reality of something that generates anxiety by blocking it from consciousness or by becoming involved in a wish-fulfilling fantasy.

Fixation: an obsessive preoccupation or attachment to something, generally the result of some traumatic experience.

Identification: a desire to become "like" someone or something in some aspect of thought or behavior.

Projection: an attempt to deny some negative or hostile feeling in oneself by attributing it to someone else. Thus a person who hates someone will "project" that hatred onto the other person, and perceive him or her as hating the original person.

Reaction formation: occurs when a pair of ambivalent attitudes generates problems, so one element is suppressed and kept unconscious by overemphasis on the other (its opposite), though it doesn't disappear. For example, a person might have ambivalent feelings of love and hatred toward another. If the hate is made unconscious and kept unconscious by the overemphasis on love, so that it appears to be replaced by love, we have a reaction formation.

Repression: unconscious instinctual wishes, memories, desires, and so on are barred from consciousness, or "repressed." This is considered the most basic defense mechanism.

Suppression: a decision is made to put something out of mind and consciousness; this is the second most basic defense mechanism. Since suppressed material is voluntarily put out of mind it can be recalled to consciousness, unlike repressed material, which is very difficult to bring to consciousness voluntarily.

Rationalization: the offerings of logical and rational reasons or excuses for behavior that is generated by unconscious and irrational determinants. The term was introduced into psychoanalysis by Ernest Jones.

Regression: the return to an earlier stage in life development when one is confronted with a stressful or anxiety-provoking situation.

Let me suggest how these defense mechanisms can be utilized by dealing with regression. In an analysis of *Pac-Man* that I have made, I contrasted *Pac-Man* with other video games that preceded it, such as *Space Invaders*. *Pac-Man* was, for more than a year, the most popular video game in America, which is one of the reasons I analyzed it.

In *Space Invaders*, one flies through the open skies zapping invading aliens. There are two things about this game that are important: one, there is freedom to fly about and two, the game is phallic. In *Pac-Man*, on the other hand, one is restricted to an enclosed area and one "attacks" by eating. In other words, aggression is oral. What we have, in *Pac-Man*, then, is a regression from the phallic (guns) to the oral (biting) as a means of fighting and a change from freedom to race around the skies to confinement in a maze. From a developmental perspective, *Pac-Man* is regressive.

The significance of this regression raises interesting questions. Regression, when it is not pathological, often involves an attempt to escape from anxiety of some kind and is a perfectly normal kind of behavior that functions "in the service of the ego." It may be that the popularity of this game suggested that, somehow, large numbers of American young people (though they weren't the only ones to play it) were experiencing anxieties which they attempted to assuage by playing *Pac-Man*. Curiously, there is often a connection between regression and fixation, so the fact that so many people played the game over and over again should not be too surprising.

Regression and the other defense mechanisms are concepts that can be applied to the behavior of characters in films, television programs and other texts and to various other aspects of the media. These concepts give us a greater understanding of human motivation and provide us with insights that enrich and deepen our ability to analyze the media.

These defense mechanisms are functions of the ego, which uses them against the id. When the id or drives threaten the ego, generating anxiety, the ego uses whatever it can to neutralize the id. There is a considerable amount of disagreement among psychoanalysts as to what can legitimately be called defense mechanisms (there are other techniques the ego has for mastering the id), but the ones I have listed are generally accepted as the most important.

DREAMS

It is possible, without stretching things too much, to make a comparison between dreams and many of the fictions brought to us by the media—especially the moving-image media, such as film and television. Dreams are like films and television productions in that they are made up of images, generally have a narrative structure (though it may be obscure and bizarre) and are frequently hard to fathom. According to Erich Fromm:

> Dreams are understood to be the hallucinatory fulfillment of irrational wishes and particularly sexual wishes which have originated in our early childhood and have not been fully transformed into reaction formations or sublimations. These wishes are expressed as being fulfilled when our conscious control is weakened, as is the case in sleep. (1957: 67)

The situation is more complicated because we don't allow ourselves to dream of certain things, which implies that some kind of a censorial agent is at work that prevents certain forbidden thoughts to appear undisguised. This is where symbols (which we've already discussed) come in—they allow us to sneak "forbidden" material by our internal censor.

Most of these symbols are sexual, as Fromm points out:

> The male genital is symbolized by sticks, trees, umbrellas, knives, pencils, hammers, airplanes, and many other objects which represent it either by their shape or by their function. The female genital is represented in the same manner by caves, bottles, boxes, doors, jewel cases, gardens, flowers, etc. Sexual pleasure is represented by activities like dancing, riding, climbing, flying. The falling out of hair or teeth is a symbolic representation of castration. Aside from sexual elements, symbols are expressive of the fundamental experiences of the little child. Father and mother are symbolized by king and queen or emperor and empress, children as little animals, death as a journey. (1957: 68-69)

It is this aspect of Freudian theory that strikes many people as "ridiculous" and that has given Freud and psychoanalytic theory such a bad name. In many cases Freud is disparaged by people who have not read him or read very little of him. To the common person, and to many others who have read a little in the field, seeing pencils and cigars as penises is simply absurd. One of the nice things about psychoanalytic theory is that this kind of behavior can be explained as repression—the refusal to acknowledge one's sexuality and other aspects of the psyche.

Many critics of Freud take comfort in quoting his statement that "Sometimes a cigar is only a cigar." This is generally employed when some Freudian interpretation of symbols is made and some object or artifact is described as a phallic symbol. I once suggested that the Washington monument, a great shaft erected in honor of the *father* of our country, is quite obviously a phallic symbol—though I don't believe that the people responsible for the monument thought of it as such. "Ha!" replied a critic, who then offered the cigar quote.

My point here is that *if "sometimes a cigar is only a cigar," other times a cigar isn't only a cigar.* You can't have it both ways. The notion that certain objects represent, to our unconscious, penises, (and other objects, of course, represent vaginas or wombs) may strike us as absurd but if you are going to argue that in some cases, suggesting something is a phallic symbol is incorrect, you must accept the notion that in other cases, suggesting something is a phallic symbol may be correct.

In any case, we find that dreams require interpretation and this must be keyed to the dreamer's life. The dreamer can help us discover a dream's true meaning by free association—revealing all thoughts that come into his or her mind—and by restructuring the dream. Fromm writes:

> This true dream, which is the expression of our hidden desires, Freud calls the "latent dream." The distorted version of the dream as we remember it is the "manifest dream" and the process of distortion and disguise is the "dream-work." The main mechanisms through which the dream-work translates the latent into the manifest dream are condensation, displacement and secondary elaboration. By condensation Freud refers to the fact that the manifest dream is much shorter than the latent dream. It leaves out a number of elements of the latent dream, combines fragments of various elements, and condenses them into one new element in the manifest dream. . . . By displacement Freud refers to the fact that an element of the latent dream, and often a very important one, is expressed by a remote element in the manifest dream and usually one which appears to be quite unimportant. (1957: 69-70)

The process of secondary elaboration involves filling in gaps in the dream, repairing inconsistencies, and so on, so the manifest dream *seems* consistent and coherent. Two things make analyzing dreams even more difficult: the fact that elements often stand for their opposites, and the fact that the manifest dream is not a coherent narrative but a series of disconnected images. Thus a dream represents a formidable problem to the analyst, who must understand how dreams disguise and distort things and be able to relate what is found in dreams to the dreamer's personal life.

A French thinker, Jacques Lacan, suggests that the semiotic concepts, metaphor and metonymy, are useful in understanding dreams. Condensation, he said, is similar to what we described in semiotics as metaphor and displacement is similar to metonymy. In condensation and in metaphor, we tie several things together; in displacement and in metonymy, we substitute one thing for something else. Lacan differed with Freud over the nature of the unconscious. Freud believed it was chaotic and pre-verbal. Lacan, on the other hand, argued "the unconscious is structured like a language," which suggested that semiotics and linguistics might be useful in understanding how the unconscious works.

Recently, some researchers have suggested that Freud's notions about dreams being responses to experiences and being based on wish-fulfillments might be inadequate. Whatever the case, his notions about how dreams function and the role that condensation and displacement play in them have interesting implications for those interested in how the media affect individuals and, by implications, society.

In the same manner much of what the media brings us can be looked upon as similar to dreams—we must look for distortions and disguises, we must concern ourselves with the unconscious and with censorship, and we must relate what we discover in the mediated work to the personal history of the dreamer, which involves both the dreamer's biography and his or her social situation. And, intervening, is the psyche of the creator and interpreters of the work of art, so the situation becomes quite complicated.

I assume here that besides the surface communication between the artist/creator and the audience/receiver there is also communication from the subconscious or unconscious of one to that of the other, so that the most important aspect of what we get from media may be submerged and not readily observable. This is why knowledge of the psyche and how it functions are so important.

AGGRESSION AND GUILT

In *Civilization and Its Discontents,* one of his last books, Freud writes about the element of aggressiveness in people:

Men are not gentle creatures who want to be loved, and who at the most can defend themselves if they are attacked; they are, on the contrary, creatures among whose instinctual endowments is to be reckoned a powerful share of aggressiveness. As a result, their neighbor is for them not only a potential helper or sexual object, but also someone who tempts them to satisfy their aggressiveness on him, to exploit his capacity for work without compensation, to use him sexually without his consent, to seize his possessions, to humiliate him, to cause him pain, to torture and to kill him. *Homo homini lupus* [man is a wolf to man]. (1962: 58)

In this passage Freud suggests that aggressiveness is instinctual, but secondary to more basic instincts. We see this when he uses the phrase "a powerful share." This aggressiveness threatens to disrupt or even destroy society and civilization as we know it, so a powerful force is brought into play. This force is guilt, which, Freud explains, is aggression turned back on itself:

Another question concerns us. . . . What means does civilization employ in order to inhibit the aggressiveness which opposes it, to make it harmless, to get rid of it, perhaps? . . . His [man's] aggressiveness is introjected, internalized; it is, in point of fact, sent back to where it came from—that is, it is directed toward his own ego. There is taken over by a portion of the ego, which sets itself over against the rest of the ego as super-ego, and which now, in the form of "conscience," is ready to put into action against the ego the same harsh aggressiveness that the ego would like to satisfy upon other, extraneous individuals. . . . Civilization, therefore, obtains mastery of the individual's dangerous desire for aggression by weakening and disarming it and by setting up an agency within him to watch over it, like a garrison in a conquered city. (1962: 70-71)

As a matter of fact, Freud argues that we are made to feel so guilty that at times we become overwhelmed with guilt and forfeit our sense of happiness. The "cost" of civilization is generally too great for us; we are forced to renounce too much (especially our sexuality) and we suffer from too much guilt.

This is where humor comes in, for humor is a means we have evolved to allow us to enjoy certain kinds of aggression by masking them and evading guilt feelings. Freud has analyzed humor in great detail in *Jokes and Their Relation to the Unconscious,* one of his most impressive works. Freud was drawn to the study of humor—a subject that has never been satisfactorily explained—because of his interest in the psyche, the unconscious, and human aggressiveness.

PSYCHOANALYTIC ANALYSIS OF MEDIA:
A CAUTIONARY NOTE

A subject as vast and complicated as the psyche poses enormous problems to a writer who wants to suggest how psychoanalytic concepts can be applied to media. As with every subject, there is always the problem of oversimplification and reductionistic thinking. In this section I have attempted to suggest to the reader how the most fundamental concepts in psychoanalytic literature can be applied to the media—how they help us to understand human motivation and perhaps how they help us to understand our reactions to what we read, see, and hear.

Because there are so many competing schools of psychoanalytic thought, and because the general public, which is not familiar with many of the concepts used by psychoanalytic thinkers, is so often hostile to these concepts, psychoanalytic criticism is a difficult pursuit. But how else can we understand the way *King Kong* or *Star Trek* or *Hamlet* (or any other work in print or film media) have the power to seize our attention and move us in profound and interesting ways?

What Simon Lesser says about literature in *Fiction and the Unconscious* can be applied to just about all media:

> The supreme virtue of psychoanalysis, from the point of view of its potential utility for literary study, is that it has investigated the very aspects of man's nature with which the greatest writers of fiction have been preoccupied: the emotional, unconscious or only partly comprehended bases of our behavior. Unlike other psychologies, but like Sophocles and Shakespeare, Tolstoy and Dostoevsky, Melville and Hawthorne, it has concerned itself with the surging, non-rational forces which play so large a part in determining our destiny as well as the part of our being which tries, often in vain, to control and direct them. It offers us a systematic and well-validated body of knowledge about those forces. (1957: 15)

Lesser moves on, then, to say something about what we would call the audience and the way it responds to fiction and media in general:

> It is my assumption that as we read we unconsciously *understand* at least some of a story's secret significance; to some extent our enjoyment is a product of this understanding. But some readers go on to try to account for the effect a story has had upon them, and to report what they discover. It is in connection with these later critical activities, which must be sharply differentiated I believe from the reading experience itself, that psychoanalytic concepts are likely to prove invaluable. They make it possible to deal

with a portion of our response which was not hitherto accessible to criticism—permit us to explain reactions which were intuitive, fugitive and often non-verbal, and supply the key to the elements in the story responsible for those reactions.

To conclude, I would like to emphasize that my purpose in this chapter has not been to provide a comprehensive review of psychoanalytic techniques, but to make a suggestion as to the usefulness of psychoanalytic criticism for understanding and interpreting both what we find carried by media and our responses to it—a suggestion worth some thought.

NOTE

1. There is also a thin area between the conscious and the unconscious known as the "preconscious," but it is not important for our immediate purposes.

ANNOTATED BIBLIOGRAPHY

Bettelheim, Bruno. *The Uses of Enchantment: The Meaning and Importance of Fairy Tales.* Vintage Books, 1977. An excellent example of the application of psychoanalytic theory (Freudian, in particular) to an important literary genre. Extended and perceptive readings of some of the most important western fairy tales appear in the second half of the book.

Brenner, Charles. *An Elementary Textbook of Psychoanalysis.* Doubleday, 1974. A classic textbook on psychoanalytic theory. Authoritative and relatively easy to read and understand.

Freud, Sigmund. *Character and Culture.* Philip Rieff, ed. Collier Books, 1963. A collection of Freud's work that focuses upon folklore, myth, literature, and the arts—that is, applications of his theories to cultural phenomena.

Freud, Sigmund. *The Interpretation of Dreams.* Avon Books. 1965. This is considered Freud's greatest book—a fascinating and controversial analysis of the nature of dreams and the role they play in our lives. Freud's discussion of symbols, condensation, displacement, distortion will be of particular interest to those interested in visual communication.

Fromm, Erich. *The Forgotten Language: An Introduction to the Understanding of Dreams, Fairy Tales and Myths.* Grove Press, 1951. An interesting study of myths and dreams with an extended comparison of the ideas of Jung and Freud.

Grotjahn, Martin. *Beyond Laughter: Humor and the Subconscious.* McGraw-Hill, 1966. A fascinating study of humor and popular culture in general that covers a lot of territory and has interesting things to say about all kinds of different topics.

Jung, Carl G. (ed.) *Man and His Symbols.* Dell, 1968. Articles by Jung and some of his followers on myths, dreams, heroic types, and other Jungian concerns. Illustrated and understandable.

Kolbenschlag, Madonna. *Kiss Sleeping Beauty Goodbye: Breaking the Spell of Feminine Myths and Models.* Doubleday. 1980. This book argues that some women have, in effect, identified too strongly with heroines from fairy tales and have not developed themselves as persons. Many wait, as in the case of Sleeping Beauty, for the perfect man to come and rescue them from lives that are boring and uneventful.

Kris, Ernst. *Psychoanalytic Explorations in Art.* Schocken, 1964. An important book on the creative process, literary criticism, the comic, and art.

Lesser, Simon O. *Fiction and the Unconscious.* Beacon Press, 1957. A psychoanalytic study of fiction that has implications for those interested in popular culture and the public arts.

Phillips, William (ed.) *Art and Psychoanalysis: Studies in the Application of Psychoanalytic Theory to the Creative Process.* Meridian Books, 1963. A collection of essays on art, literature, and the creative process, psychological criticism, and related matters.

Rank, Otto. *The Double: A Psychoanalytic Study.* Meridien Books. 1979. A fascinating study of the double motif (doppleganger) as it is found in myths and literary and artistic texts.

Spector, Jack J. *The Aesthetics of Freud: A Study in Psychoanalysis and Art.* McGraw-Hill, 1974. A study of Freud's theories of art and of his influence on art and literature, with attention paid to biographical matters.

4

SOCIOLOGICAL ANALYSIS

Much of the debate about media in contemporary society has a sociological dimension, so in this chapter we deal, first, with sociological concepts that have the most immediate applicability to media analysis. This is followed by a discussion of "uses and gratifications" theory and a listing and explanation of a number of suggested uses and gratifications connected to media. Finally we deal with content analysis and suggest a simple content analysis exercise that will yield interesting results.

Someone once defined a sociologist as a person "who tells everyone things they already know in language they can't understand." I use the term "sociological" here in the broadest sense possible. My focus will be on social relationships of men and women, in contrast, for example, to psychological matters such as the consciousness of individuals. We will examine the public arts with a concern for human interactions and personal relationships, asking ourselves, "Who does what to whom and why?" and "What patterns do we find in the material we study?"

It is useful to differentiate sociology from other social sciences such as anthropology, political science, and psychology by looking at their core concepts. The basic concern in sociology is how groups and institutions function. Institutions are generally understood to be ways of patterning and organizing social life. The core concepts of psychology, as I mentioned earlier, are the individual psyche and the unconscious. For anthropologists, the core concept is culture and for political scientists, the core concepts are power and government. These disciplines are often combined, so we have social psychologists, political sociologists, social anthropologists, and so on.

The term "sociology" was coined by French philosopher Auguste Comte (1798-1857), who conceived of it as a means of integrating theoretical and practical knowledge about human beings. The purpose of sociology was, Comte said, "to know in order to predict in order to control." Comte wanted to discover the laws by which people lived so a rational and humane social order could be established. Since Comte, sociology has evolved and we find sociologists studying everything from collective behavior, deviance, and religion to the way bureaucracies function and how social change occurs.

In this chapter I will deal with three areas. First, I will discuss some of the basic concepts sociologists use when they study society. These concepts will provide us with tools for analysis and will enable us to see things we might have neglected previously. For example, take the concept of roles. It is only recently that media critics have paid much attention to the roles given to women in films and television programs, and to related matters such as the number of women relative to the number of men, the age of these women, and what happens to them. Knowing some of the more important sociological concepts will enable us to analyze media in a way somewhat different from the ways we've previously analyzed it.

A second approach I will discuss is one that deals with the gratifications the public arts offer to people and the needs they help people deal with. In recent years there has been a good deal of interest in this "needs and gratifications" approach (sometimes also called "uses and gratifications"). The focus here is on how people *use* the media and what gratifications it offers them. I will offer a number of suggested needs and gratifications that can be applied to the public arts and that will help us understand why certain programs are so popular as well as what role they might play in society.

Finally, I will deal with a standard sociological technique, content analysis, which uses statistical techniques to make inferences about what is found in the media. Let's take the matter of violence on children's television programs as an example. Once we decide upon a working definition of violence, we can examine a sampling of children's television programs and count the incidents of violence we find. This enables us to move from saying, "There's a lot of violence on children's television," to something like "There are X incidents of violence per hour on children's television."

Frequently content analysis adopts a historical frame of reference and examines, for instance, earlier samples of children's programs in order to make comparisons. Using content analysis techniques, we can determine whether there is more violence in childrens' television programs now than there was at some earlier time. If there is more violence now, what does that mean?

SOME BASIC CONCEPTS

In this section I list some of the most fundamental concepts used in sociology that can be applied to the public arts. I've tried to explain them as concisely as I can; I hope that in my effort to be clear I have not oversimplified matters too greatly.

Alienation. This means, literally, "no ties," and refers to a feeling of estrangement and separation from others. A person who is alienated feels like "a stranger" (alien) with no connections to his or her society or to some group in that society.

This feeling of alienation is connected, in many instances, to the bureaucracies that develop in organizations. Bureaucracies are often necessary to deal with large numbers of people in a fair and efficient manner, but they are also impersonal and generate feelings of alienation. Students in large universities are frequently known to the administration only by their social security numbers and our language about students also has an alienating tone. We sometimes talk about young men and women as being "college material."

We can use the concept of alienation to understand the behavior of characters in texts—Willy Loman in *Death of a Salesman*—and of social groups and sub-cultures—teenagers, punk rockers, etc. When we use this concept we must connect it, very specifically, to acts of characters and the behavior of groups and subcultures.

Anomie. This word is derived from the Greek word *nomos,* meaning norms. A person who rejects the norms of a given society is described as anomic. Anomie and alienation are quite different. A group of thieves might have a strong sense of fellowship and thus not be alienated. But because they have no respect for the laws of society, they would be described as anomic.

Bureaucracy. As society becomes larger and more complex, it becomes increasingly difficult to regulate, and keeping things running with any degree of efficiency can be a problem. Bureaucracies are collections of more or less anonymous people who follow fixed rules and routines in running organizations. There is usually a hierarchy of authority, impersonal handling of problems, and a great deal of red tape.

Class (socioeconomic). A class is a group of people with something in common. When we use the term sociologically, we usually mean socioeconomic class, which refers to a person's class level or place in the hierarchy of classes that exists in society. W. Lloyd Warner, a distinguished sociologist and anthropologist, has suggested there are six classes in American society: upper-upper, lower-upper, upper-middle, lower-middle, upper-lower, and lower-lower. Warner's estimates (published a number of years ago) of the distribution of these classes in the United States are as follows:

upper-upper—1.4% of the population
lower-upper—1.6% of the population
upper-middle—10% of the population
lower-middle—28% of the population
upper-lower—33% of the population
lower-lower—25% of the population

Warner suggests that the lower-middle and upper-lower classes constitute the "common man" level. These figures are somewhat outdated, but they give an idea of the class makeup of American society that is still fairly accurate.

Socioeconomic class is determined by a number of components, such as education, income, and occupation, and different social classes have different lifestyles, ways of raising children, and values.

It is estimated that the wealthiest 1% of American families own more than 40% of all the corporate stock in the country and the top 10% own almost 70% of the total wealth. This 10% owns around half the value of all real estate and more than 90% of business corporate stocks and business assets and bonds. We have approximately 80 million families in America, but 400,000 households own 27% of the wealth. These figures were compiled in the early 1980s and since then the concentration of wealth has increased. The lowest tenth percent of American families have been losing ground, economically.

Thus, although we tend to think of ourselves as an essentially "classless, all-middle class" society, we are actually very much a class-based society. We do have a substantial middle class, but there is very definitely an economic elite in the United States which has enormous political power.

Deviance. Deviance refers to behavioral patterns that are different from typical or conventional ones (and some would say normal ones).

Our attitudes toward different deviants change over time. Thus homosexuality was once considered criminal but now is defined as deviant and tolerated by most people. Deviance generates anxiety in people because it forces us to consider how valid our practices are and how correct our attitudes are about what is normal.

Elites. This term refers to people at the top of the social pyramid, the upper-class and lower-upper-class people who have positions of power, who are affluent, and who generally have professional and executive occupations. (The opposite of the elites would be the common man and common woman.) It has been documented that television heroes tend to be relatively young, well-educated, white professionals; there are very few working-class heroes. We might wonder what effect this overrepresentation of elites has on people.

Ethnicity. This is conventionally understood to mean groups existing in a society that share certain cultural traits and traditions that distinguish them. Thus Italians, Poles, Germans, Finns, Jews (who are a special case), and countless other groups are all considered to be ethnics. For many years ethnics tried to camouflage their identity in America, but lately ethnics have become proud of their heritages and are no longer trying to escape their roots. Ethnic groups are often stereotyped in the media, though this practice is now under attack.

Functionalism. Sociologists say something is *functional* when it contributes to the maintenance and stability of whatever entity it is part of; likewise, something is *disfunctional* (or *dysfunctional*) if it is a destabilizing or destructive factor. If it has no effect on the entity it is part of, it is called "nonfunctional. What complicates matters is that something may be functional in some regards and disfunctional in other regards at the same time. Thus television in general may be functional in that it provides a great deal of information to people, helps fuel consumption, and stresses certain values, but it may be disfunctional in that it provides negative roles for many people, suggests that the world is more violent than it really is, and creates feelings of anxiety and discontent in people who cannot afford all of the good (and bad) things advertised on television. There is a conservative bias to functional analysis in that it emphasizes the maintenance and stability of society, instead of focusing on changes that might be made.

We can also examine phenomena in terms of whether or not their functions are intended or unintended, conscious or unconscious. Thus the *manifest function* of news programs might be to inform people, while the *latent function* of these programs might be to indoctrinate people with certain political values and beliefs. The reporters and newscasters, I should point out, may not be aware that they are indoctrinating people; they may believe that all they are doing is reporting the news.

As media analysts, we are interested in the roles individual performers play in texts and in the roles assigned to women, ethnic and racial minorities, old and young people, and representatives of other groups (sexual, political, religious, socio-economic) as well. Viewers of films and television programs often identify with the heroes and heroines in these texts and use them to create identities. There is, many believe, a considerable amount of "social teaching" that is generated by the media.

Many critics argue that the roles that women play in the media are demeaning. They are treated, all too often, only as sexual objects, used for display or as dummies who get excited about some brand of toilet paper. They are seldom portrayed as professionals who can be productive and should be taken seriously. Frequently, they are not shown as active, but rather as passive figures who react to the initiatives of others, usually males.

These roles give people very destructive images about what women are like and how they should be treated and have negative consequences not only for women, but for men as well. I could also discuss the way Blacks, Asians, Latinos, Jews, the handicapped, and countless others are portrayed in the media.

When we look at roles from a sociological perspective, then, we must ask ourselves about the roles that are assigned people (who must be seen as representatives of social groups) and what impact these roles might have upon individuals and society, in general.

There is one other concept that is of interest—*functional alternatives*. Sociologists use this idea to explain situations in which, for example, an original institution loses its viability (to some extent) and is replaced by a substitute institution. According to functionalist theory, institutions are created and evolve because certain things have to be done to keep a society operating properly. If the original institution no longer works, something must be found to take its place.

Let us assume, for example, that people have a need for some kind of religious experience, some form of connection with powers beyond the human. This need, in America, was taken care of by organized religions. But as mainline organized religions have lost popularity, something else was needed to take their place, and what evolved was professional football. Professional football might be seen, from this perspective, as a functional alternative to organized religion. (This matter is discussed in more detail in the chapter on football in the Applications section.)

All of these different aspects of functional analysis are summarized in the list that follows:

> *functional:* maintains an organization, society, or the like
> *disfunctional:* destabilizes an organization, society, or the like
> *nonfunctional:* plays no role
> *manifest function:* intended and recognized by people
> *latent function:* not intended and not recognized by people
> *functional alternative:* substitutes for original institution, practice

Lifestyle. Here we have a comprehensive term that covers a person's tastes in fashion, cars, entertainment and recreation, literature, and related matters. "Style" suggests fashion, and the term "lifestyle" describes how a person fashions his or her life. Lifestyle is often connected to socioeconomic class, and is reflected in a person's "image."

Lifestyle is reflected in various kinds of taste decisions: the kind of car one drives, in the kind of dog or cat one has, in the magazines one reads (or, at least, has on the coffee table), in where one lives, what one's house is like (how big, the color of the walls, the kind of furniture), what one does for a living, what kind of food one eats and what restaurants one goes to, what kind of vacations one takes . . . the list is endless. All of these phenomena tend to be class specific and are reflections of one's class and so-called level of sophistication. The institution which tutors us about these matters is advertising, one of whose basic functions is to make sure, to the extent it can, that "expenditure always rises to meet, if not exceed, income."

Race. David Dressler (1969: 518-519) defines race as *"a category of people with a common genetic heritage"* and mentions that physical anthropologists "often cited three broad classifications of race: *Negroid, Mongoloid* and *Caucasoid* (although other divisions are sometimes listed)." Race, it must be added, is not the same thing as ethnicity, which is connected to nationality and not genetic makeup. I mention the subject of race because there has been a considerable amount of racism in the public arts, historically, and it is still a problem.

Role (social). We know what a role is in a play, and the concept of social roles is very similar. It refers to certain kinds of behavior that we learn, that relate to expectations people have of us, that are connected to specific situations, and that are determined, in part, by our place in society. In the course of a day the average individual plays many roles: parent, worker, companion, and so on.

Sex (gender). Sex is an important sociological concept when it is linked to roles and some of the other terms discussed here. Many media critics argue that the media have given women destructive sex roles, or images, and are "sexist." This is certainly an important matter to keep in mind when analyzing the media.

A content analysis ("Magazine's Heroines: Is *Ms.* Just Another Member of the *Family Circle*?) made by sociologist E. Barbara Phillips is most instructive. She analyzed random selections of two magazines— *Ms.* and *Family Circle*—and discovered considerable differences between them.

The women who were the subjects of articles in *Family Circle* were homemakers and there were no articles about women who were involved in politics or social concerns. The articles in *Ms.,* on the other hand, didn't deal with any women as homemakers (though many of them were married and had families) but were focused on the way these women were involved in social, cultural and political life, and public service. The two magazines projected different roles for women and, no doubt, helped support and reinforce the value systems of the women reading each publication.

Socialization. This refers to the process by which people are taught the rules, roles, and values of their society. We may look upon socialization as a kind of indoctrination that is done formally through institutions, such as the family, the school system, and the church, and informally through the media. What is important about informal socialization is that we generally do not recognize that we are being taught (some would say programmed) what roles to play and how to play them, what values to espouse, what attitudes to have, what goals to strive for, and so on.

Status. Status is often confused with role; the two are actually quite different, though one is connected with the other. Status involves the position a person has in some group or organization and the prestige that is connected with this position. It is associated with a person's role. Within universities, for example, full professors have more status than assistant professors and play different roles. Within society in general those who have certain occupations have great status (doctors, lawyers, professors, bankers) and others have little status (ditch diggers). Status or prestige is a powerful force in society that is used to control people in subtle ways.

Stereotype. In Horton and Hunt's *Sociology* (1972: 163), stereotype is defined as "*a group-shared image of another group or category of people.* Stereotypes can be positive (the kindly, dedicated family doctor), negative (the unprincipled, opportunistic politician) or mixed (the dedicated, fussy, sexless, old-maid school teacher)." Regardless of whether stereotypes are positive or negative, they are very dangerous.

They give millions of people oversimplified, erratic, and sometimes pernicious images of Blacks, Jews, Frenchmen, doctors, police officers, women—the list could be endless. No matter what the form—racial stereotyping, occupational stereotyping, sex-role stereotyping, or some other—stereotypes are oversimplifications and overgeneralizations that minimize individual differences; they tend to be very destructive.

Values. This refers to attitudes people have relative to what is desirable and undesirable, good and bad. Our values, in indirect ways, affect our behavior and cover a wide spectrum of social phenomena: sex, politics, education, and so on. As media critics we must concern ourselves with the values of the characters we see in dramatic productions and with what these values suggest about our society.

This minicourse in sociological concepts is meant to alert you to some of the concerns sociologists (and other social scientists, as well) have and what they look at when they examine the public arts. As I pointed out in some of my discussions of these concepts, frequently it is useful to combine the concepts and consider such matters as sex-role stereotyping, socio economic class and status, racism and sexism (and all the other isms), the values of deviants, and so forth. The student interested in exploring these concepts in more detail and within the structure of sociological theory in general should consult any of the standard introductory texts to sociology. Also, at the end of this chapter an annotated bibliography of some important books that take a "media sociology" approach is provided.

I should point out here, and this makes matters complicated, that we are dealing with works of art when we analyze sitcoms, soap operas, commercials, and all the other genres carried in the public arts. We should not consider them to be *merely* documents to be examined in terms of their sociological content; we must take other considerations into account, such as artistic conventions and the difficulties involved in dealing with some artistic or creative personalities.

USES AND GRATIFICATIONS

There is a good deal of controversy related to "uses and gratifications" theory, but the same can be said about every other theory that deals with media. Despite the fact that much research on media has been of an empirical nature and concerned with the effects media have on attitudes (and many other matters), there has been a considerable amount of interest in the ways people use media and the gratifications media offer to people. Katz et al. mention some works about the subject:

Herzog (1942) on quiz programs and the gratifications derived from listening to soap operas; Suchman (1942) on the motives for getting interested in serious music on radio; Wolfe and Fiske (1949) on the development of children's interest in comics; Berelson (1949) on the functions of newspaper reading; and so on. Each of these investigations came up with a list of functions served either by some specific contents or by the medium in question: to match one's wits against others, to get information or advice for daily living, to provide a framework for one's day, to prepare oneself culturally for the demands of upward mobility, or to be reassured about the dignity and usefulness of one's role. (1979: 215)

Regardless of whether you think that soap operas are stupid or that situation comedies are silly, the *functions* that these programs—and others—perform for people may in some cases be quite important.

In the material that follows I will list and briefly describe a number of suggested gratifications that the media offer and needs that they help assuage. There is a good deal of scientific work that remains to be done on our needs, on the gratifications we seek, and on the role media play here, but it seems quite obvious that people do use media (though they may not be aware of the fact that they are doing so) in varying ways.

The material in the list that follows comes from a number of different sources, but I am particularly indebted to my colleague, Stuart Hyde, who has dealt with a number of needs and desires people have and the way the public arts deal with them.

It is difficult to decide, in some cases, whether we are dealing with a need, a use, a gratification, or a desire, so I've avoided these terms altogether and leave that for you to determine. The list is also incomplete; you may be able to add important topics to it that will help you to understand more fully how the media function.

(1) To be amused. We seem to want to be entertained, to find things to laugh about, to be put in a happy spirit. This is a source of positive pleasure.

(2) To see authority figures exalted or deflated. America is a society with egalitarian values, and Americans tend to regard authority as invalid. Thus we like to see authority figures deflated and ridiculed, especially politicians, soldiers, professors, and psychiatrists. There are some authority figures we tend to exalt, however: clergymen, surgeons, and detectives, to name a few. The media play an important role in teaching us how to relate to authority and deal with authority figures.

(3) To experience the beautiful. We give high status to beautiful music, beautiful works of art, and people who are physically attractive, in particular, beautiful women. What is beautiful is another matter, however, and our definitions of beauty change over the years.

(4) To have shared experiences with others (community). One of the more important functions of the mass media is to give people a common cultural (or pop cultural) frame of reference. In some cases, such as when we go to football games in huge stadiums, we are actually with others in a momentary kind of community. And this experience is often shared with millions of others who may listen to the game on the radio or watch it on television. In other cases we merely watch a program "along with" millions of others. It has been discovered that one of the most important topics of conversation is media, so sharing the same programs or films helps people relate to one another.

(5) To satisfy curiosity and be informed. This has to do with our wish to know what's going on, to be up to date on things, to follow stories as they develop, and that kind of thing. The satisfaction of curiosity probably has to do with nosiness and a natural inquisitiveness we seem to have, while the desire to know what's going on and to be informed has to do with surveillance and the anxiety we feel when we are "in the dark." One thing is certain—we learn a great deal from the media both directly and indirectly.

(6) To identify with the deity and the divine plan. Many people have some form of what might be called "the God concept," and the media often help people gain a sense of the nature of life, the power of spiritual forces, and so forth.

(7) To find distraction and diversion. Many people find that the public arts help them escape (if only momentarily) from worry and anxiety and help them pass the time when they are bored. This kind of thing is sometimes described as "killing time" by those who feel the public arts tend to be mindless and destructive, but from our uses and gratifications perspective, the public arts never allow us only to "kill time." We may *seem* to be doing nothing (and even think we are doing nothing) when we watch television or listen to rock music, but in truth a great deal is going on.

(8) To experience empathy. By this I mean being able to share in the joys and sorrows of others and deriving, from this, psychological pleasure—often catharsis or "relief." Although we relate to the various characters we see in the media vicariously, we still are able to share in their emotional experiences and this enriches us greatly. It also helps us prepare ourselves emotionally for the difficulties we all face in real life at one time or another.

(9) To experience, in a guilt-free and controlled situation, extreme emotions, such as love and hate, the horrible and the terrible, and similar phenomena. This is slightly different from experiencing empathy, which involves identifying with characters. Here I'm talking about

our desire to experience powerful emotions without being carried away by them or feeling guilt about them. The media enable us to have powerful experiences without paying for them, so to speak, and to take risks without having to worry about being devastated. (There is some question, however, as to whether we do escape from being affected by our media experiences. Despite the "controls," we may end up having various morbid residues, triggerings to violence, and so on that we are unaware of consciously, but that may trouble us.)

(10) To find models to imitate. These models help us to gain a sense of identity, teach us how to cope in certain situations, and, informally, socialize us. One problem here is that we may identify with villains rather than heroes and heroines and pick up ideas, attitudes, and behavior patterns that are harmful and destructive. For example, there is a great deal of fear that children who watch cartoon programs full of violence will learn to be violent and to use violence as a means of solving problems.

(11) To gain an identity. An identity can be defined as a coherent sense of self, a personal style, a "defined" personality. We are no longer a traditional society, and as our traditions wither, as we become more mobile, modern, and materialistic, we find it increasingly more difficult to gain an identity. This is where the media come in—and, in particular, the various heroic and unheroic figures we follow in the comics, watch on television, read about in popular novels, and so on. They help us manufacture identities, so to speak. But whether or not these identities are suitable, long lasting, and good for us is another matter.

(12) To gain information about the world. In some cases this is obvious: we hear economists talk about economic problems, professors are called upon to explain things to us, documentaries deal with topics of interest, and, at times, courses are actually taught on television. But we also learn a great deal "incidentally" all the time. This incidental learning involves some matters I've already mentioned—learning how to behave in certain situations, finding heroic figures to emulate, and having certain values reinforced. The media are always teaching us something, even when they are not intentionally doing so, and even when we don't realize they are doing so. A good question we might keep in mind, then, is, "What are we learning from the media?"

(13) To reinforce our belief in justice. It doesn't always work out this way, but generally speaking we like to see heroes defeat villains and to see evil punished and virtue rewarded. In other words, we want to believe that the universe is moral and that crime doesn't pay.

(14) To believe in romantic love. Although our belief in the power of love may be waning, we still tend to see romantic love as a wonderful

thing and as a prime motivating force in relationships. Implicit in the belief in romantic love is the notion that our emotions are powerful forces that are capable, at times, of overwhelming logic, reason, class differences, age differences, racial differences, and anything else. We also believe that romantic love doesn't always lead to happiness.

(15) To believe in magic, the marvelous, and the miraculous. This belief, which probably stems in great measure from childhood (fairy tales, seeing magicians, and so on), explains our interest in horror, science fiction, and the like. It also represents a way of dealing with the demonic.

(16) To see others make mistakes. "To err is human," it has been said, and we all do make mistakes. When we see others make the same or similar mistakes as us, we feel less guilty or upset, since we can conclude that it is perfectly natural to make mistakes. In certain instances we also gain a sense of superiority, since we weren't "stupid" enough to make *that* mistake. In addition, we can also learn by watching others make mistakes and pay for them—mistakes that we can try to avoid.

(17) To see order imposed on the world. We want to believe that the universe makes sense, that things have reasons for being the way they are, and that we can plan ahead. The media constantly help us gain a sense of the orderliness of the world by teaching us about such things as the laws of nature, human psychology and motivation, and social phenomena.

(18) To participate in history (vicariously). We all want to be on the scene when important events take place—to be there when the big ball games are played, to hear what politicians have to say when history is being made—and the media help us do this. We can even spend our evenings overhearing (so to speak) celebrities chatter about their love lives. I would argue that this desire to "participate" in history is a powerful force in our lives and reflects our feelings of alienation and insignificance. Television allows the nobodies, huddled in front of their sets, to watch the somebodies on the talk shows.

(19) To be purged of unpleasant emotions. The public arts often provide for a catharsis or purgation of our emotions through art. We can find ways of discharging anger, anxiety, hostility, and a host of other negative feelings by watching plays, football games, movies, listening to music, and so on. Some public art forms, such as soap operas and professional wrestling, provide us with clearly defined "hate" figures to help with this purgation.

(20) To obtain outlets for our sexual drives in a guilt-free context. In recent years a number of people and groups have attacked the allegedly

excessive amount of violence on television. This has led television (and other media, as well) to find other ways of attracting and maintaining audience interest. One of these is humor and the other is sex. Sexuality is treated much more explicitly in films than on television, where everything tends to be implied but where "wiggle and jiggle" or "tits and ass" now are major elements in programming. Our sexual experiences are always vicarious ones when it comes to media. Whether these vicarious experiences provide relief or generate anxiety and negative feelings (because, for example, our wives or girl friends are not beauty queens and sex goddesses) is a matter for conjecture.

(21) *To explore taboo subjects with impunity and without risk.* Because media allows us to examine taboo subjects "from a distance," we are able to obtain double benefits. We can explore the subject and derive whatever excitement or titillation it may generate, and we can gain a sense of moral satisfaction by condemning it or coming to some kind of a conclusion about it. When the media examine, either dramatically or in documentaries, topics such as incest, homosexuality, rape, drug abuse, or child beating (to name just a few topics) we get the "thrill" of finding out about these subjects and the reward of being able to condemn them.

(22) *To experience the ugly.* This is the opposite side of our desire to experience the beautiful. People have always been fascinated with ugliness, grotesques, and monsters in a rather complex way. We are both attracted and repelled by ugliness. I should also point out here that our attitudes toward what is beautiful and ugly change over the years and this further complicates the matter.

(23) *To affirm moral, spiritual, and cultural values.* Values are beliefs we have (which we learn from our families, friends, religions, and other institutions) about what is good and bad, what is desirable and undesirable, what is just and unjust. They deal with our actions and conduct, and tend to be "ultimate." That is, they are the bedrock upon which we build our lives and societies. Two of the more important values in American society are egalitarianism and achievement. We may not have always put these values into practice but they are goals toward which we work.

The media tend to reinforce certain values and neglect others. When we examine media we must be mindful of the values we find and consider whether they are positive or negative, why they are being championed, and what they tell us about our social order.

(24) *To see villains in action.* Villains are often more interesting than heroes and heroines, who must be good, moral, and thoughtful—at least most of the time. (The matter isn't quite so simple now, since we often

find "good-bad" heroes and "bad-good" villains.) Villains can do all kinds of things, have much more room for their maneuvering, and can be of all sorts and natures. We like to see all the terrible things they are capable of doing, but we also like to see them punished. This gives us two satisfactions for the price of one.

The list below provides a summary of the uses and gratifications of the media we have just discussed.

(1) to be amused
(2) to see authority figures exalted or deflated
(3) to experience the beautiful
(4) to have shared experiences with others
(5) to satisfy curiosity and be informed
(6) to identify with the deity and the divine plan
(7) to find distraction and diversion
(8) to experience empathy
(9) to experience, in a guilt-free situation, extreme emotions
(10) to find models to imitate
(11) to gain an identity
(12) to gain information about the world
(13) to reinforce our belief in justice
(14) to believe in romantic love
(15) to believe in magic, the marvelous, and the miraculous
(16) to see others make mistakes
(17) to see order imposed on the world
(18) to participate in history (vicariously)
(19) to be purged of unpleasant emotions
(20) to obtain outlets for our sexual drives in a guilt-free context
(21) to explore taboo subjects with impunity
(22) to experience the ugly
(23) to affirm moral, spiritual, and cultural values
(24) to see villains in action

When you analyze a text from a uses and gratifications point of view, try to determine which uses and gratifications are most important and which are secondary. Also, be sure that you can cite an event in the text (some event in a film, situation comedy, soap opera, comic book) for each use or gratification you see being taken care of. That is, you should have some justification for your assertions.

One problem with the uses and gratifications approach is that different critics often see the same event (in a film, for instance) as being used in different ways or as providing different gratifications. This is because uses and gratifications are somewhat ambiguous. But the uses and gratifications approach helps us to understand the power media have. One question we must continually keep in mind when we think about the public arts is this—they do a great deal *for* us, but what are they doing *to* us?

CONTENT ANALYSIS

Content analysis is a research technique based upon measuring (counting) the amount of something (violence, percentages of Blacks, women, professional types, or whatever) in a random sampling of some forms of communication (such as comics, sitcoms, soap operas, news shows). The basic assumption implicit in content analysis is that an investigation of messages and communication gives insights into the people who receive these messages.

An early content analysis of magazines is instructive. It was made by sociologist Leo Lowenthal and dealt with "biographies in popular magazines." Lowenthal studied biographies of popular heroes that were found in two magazines: *Collier's* and *The Saturday Evening Post*. He classified the biographies in terms of whether they dealt with political life, business and the professions, or entertainment.

He discovered some interesting things. First, there was an increase in the number of biographies over the years. Second, the number of articles on politicians and business/professionals declined and the number of articles on entertainers increased. And the articles on entertainers changed from being about serious artists and writers to popular entertainers of one sort or another.

Lowenthal suggests that the earlier biographical articles focused on "idols of production" (providing education and orientation) and the later articles focused on "idols of consumption" such as movie stars and other entertainment figures. They dealt with what we would describe now as the lifestyle preferences and consumption patterns of these figures. Lowenthal went on to discuss how these "idols of consumption" related to matters such as our attitudes toward childhood, success, adjustment, and the socializing function of these biographies. (His article is 40 pages long and is frequently cited by sociologists.)

The advantages of content analysis are:

It is inexpensive.
It is usually relatively easy to get material.

It is unobtrusive (and thus doesn't influence people).

It yields data that can be quantified.

It can deal with current events or past events, or both.

The difficulties with content analysis are:

It is hard to be certain that the sample studied is representative.

It is often hard to obtain a good working definition of the topic being studied (for example, what is violence?).

It isn't easy to find a measurable unit such as a frame in a comic strip. What does one do about films or magazine articles?

It isn't possible to prove that the inferences made on the basis of a content analysis are correct.

Despite the difficulties involved with making content analyses, it is possible to conduct interesting and useful experiments with this research technique. The secret is to choose a medium that is relatively easy to deal with, which is why we will be analyzing comics.

In terms of content analysis, comics have a number of advantages. Most of us are familiar with them, their characters are easily classifiable, they are easy to obtain, and they are easy to work with. Unlike the electronic media, which flit by us rapidly, the comics stay stuck on the page and we can spend as much time analyzing them as we wish.

We choose our categories on the basis of what it is we want to discover. Let me suggest some topics we might want to consider:

physical characteristics of heroes and heroines, villains and villainesses

color of hair	age
color of eyes	body structure
height	sex
weight	race

social aspects of characters

occupation	status
education	role
religion	ethnic background (nationality)
socioeconomic class	

emotional nature of characters

warm or cold	powerful or weak
anxious or calm	loving or hateful
stable or unstable	individualist or conformist

authoritarian or dependent   vivacious or apathetic
hostile or friendly

This list suggests some of the matters we might concern ourselves with in a content analysis of the comics that focuses on the characters in these stories. We must also keep in mind thematic matters, such as the amount of violence (and its use), the values of the characters, allusions to social and political events, reflections of cultural matters, and similar phenomena.

There is one other aspect of content analysis that should be mentioned here and that is that content analyses are most useful when they have a historic or comparative dimension to them. While it is interesting to know, for example, how much violence there is in the daily newspaper's comics pages, it is even more interesting to know how much violence there was in the daily newspaper's comics pages ten years ago, twenty years ago, thirty years ago, and so on. By taking a historical point of view we can determine *trends* and see whether there have been significant changes in our attitudes about (or stereotypes of) women, Blacks, ethnic groups—or any of the other topics listed above. By taking a comparative point of view we can see how our values and beliefs differ from those in another culture or society.

An interesting exercise in content analysis would be to choose a comic page from some newspaper (making sure it is on microfilm) and deal with it in terms of the topics listed above as well as in terms of strips, the average number of characters per frame, the percentage of male and female characters on the page, the number of words spoken by male and female characters, and the number of acts of violence. Make a comparison between what you find on the present-day page of comics and what you find on the comics page of the same paper twenty, thirty, or forty years ago (this is why it is helpful for it to be on microfilm).

With this discussion of content analysis I bring to a conclusion my introduction to sociological perspectives on the media. It is, at best, a start, but it should provide you with a sense of the kinds of things sociologists look for when they examine media and the public arts. There is a degree of overlap with Marxist analysis here that might be expected, since Marxist concepts inform a good deal of sociological thought. The uses and gratifications approach also has psychological dimensions.

ANNOTATED BIBLIOGRAPHY

Arens, W. and Susan P. Montague. *The American Dimension: Cultural Myths and Social Realities*. Alfred, 1976. A collection of articles on foods, films, football, fast foods, soaps, etc. written from an anthropological perspective.

Berger, Arthur Asa. *The TV-Guided American*. Walker & Co. 1976. This book analyzes a number of television shows (*All In The Family, Kung Fu, Mission Impossible,* etc.) in terms of what they reflect about American culture and society.

Berger, Arthur Asa. (ed.) *Television in Society*. Transaction Books. 1987. A collection of essays originally published in *Society* magazine on television shows, media events, and various social aspects of television.

Berger, Arthur Asa. *Media Research Techniques*. Sage. 1991. This book describes and assists readers in carrying out a number of research projects involving the media such as content analysis, focus groups, and the rhetorical analysis of magazine advertisements.

Berger, Peter L. and Brigitte Berger. *Sociology: A Biographical Approach*. Basic Books, 1972. An innovative textbook of sociology that focuses on the great thinkers of the discipline and their basic ideas.

Burns, Elizabeth and Tom Burns (eds.) *Sociology of Literature and Drama*. Penguin, 1973. A collection of essays by some of the more important thinkers of the contemporary period. Written from a sociological point of view, though Marxist and structuralist thinkers are also included.

McLuhan, Marshall. *The Mechanical Bride: Folklore of Industrial Man*. Beacon, 1976. A brilliant study of the sociological significance of American advertisements and comics. A pioneering effort that still is worth careful attention.

Real, Michael R. *Mass-Mediated Culture*. Prentice-Hall, 1977. Studies of Disney, the Super Bowl, *Marcus Welby* and Billy Graham, along with material of theoretical importance.

Rosenberg, Bernard and David Manning White (eds.) *Mass Culture: The Popular Arts in America*. Free Press, 1957. One of the earliest and most important collections of articles on the subject.

Tuchman, Gaye, Arlene Kaplan Daniels, and James Benét (eds.) *Hearth and Home: Images of Women in the Mass Media*. Oxford University Press, 1978. Articles on images of women in television and women's magazines with an extensive annotated bibliography on the subject.

Weibel, Kathryn. *Mirror Mirror: Images of Women Reflected in Popular Culture*. Anchor Books. 1977. This book deals with images of women found in fiction, television, the movies, women's magazines, print advertising and fashion.

Wilson, Robert N. (ed.) *The Arts in Society*. Prentice-Hall, 1964. While focused on high culture, it provides some excellent articles, including two works by Ian Watt (on Robinson Crusoe and literature and society).

Winick, Charles. *The New People: Desexualization in American Life*. Pegasus, 1968. A study of desexualization that deals with many aspects of popular culture and leaves the reader with a great deal to think about. Controversial, wide-ranging, fascinating.

II

APPLICATIONS

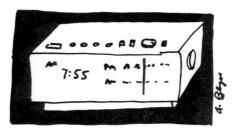

5

MURDERERS ON THE ORIENT EXPRESS

Murder on the Orient Express **and classical murder mysteries in general are examined in this chapter from semiological and Marxist points of view. First we discuss how Christie violates the "code" of the single murderer and suggest that mysteries are, in fact, problems in applied semiology that we seldom can solve because we either neglect or misinterpret the signifiers (clues) that are provided for us. We then discuss elements of class conflict found in mysteries and the role these works may play in diverting people's attention and mystifying them. Finally we suggest that, ironically, mysteries may have a revolutionary element implicit in their structure.**

Murder on the Orient Express is generally considered to be one of Agatha Christie's best works and a classic in the analytical detective mystery genre. It was also made into a highly successful movie that used the story primarily as a vehicle for cameo roles by major stars such as Lauren Bacall and Ingrid Bergman, but which also was beautifully acted and wonderfully absorbing.

What is distinctive about this particular story is that, unlike in most mysteries, *all* of the suspects were the actual murderers. And once Hercule Poirot figured this out, everything else fell beautifully into place—as things must in a well-constructed mystery. A mystery story is, semiologically speaking, like a coded message. All kinds of signs and significations are observable, but the connections among them are not obvious. Once we see how they are related and "break the code," so to speak, the mystery is solved. Clues, then, are signifiers with a number of different signifieds. We must assemble these clues and interpret them properly to make sense of things and find the killer(s).

In *Murder on the Orient Express*, having a dozen suspects all guilty was a remarkable and ingenious structural innovation, a reversal of the conventional situation in which only one suspect is guilty. The fascination with the movie lay in seeing how Poirot put everything together. Many of the people who saw the film probably had read the book; they wanted to see it actualized in the film—to see it "come alive," reinterpreted, and that is what they got.

ORGANIZING A MYSTERY

If we forget (to the extent this is possible) about the actual plot and examine the story in terms of characters and relationships, we find that *Murder on the Orient Express* has a very symmetrical organization. There are three main characters or, rather, two polarly opposite characters and a group of a dozen other interrelated characters who form a third character and who mediate between the first two. We find Poirot, the detective, on one side and Ratchett (an alias for a kidnapper, Cassetti) on the other. By chance Poirot happens to board the Orient Express on his way back to France with Ratchett and a dozen other people. Poirot is recognized by Ratchett, who offers him twenty thousand dollars to protect him because he's received some death threats. But Poirot feels that Ratchett is an evil man and has taken an immediate and instinctive dislike to him, and so refuses.

Ratchett looks "evil" and Poirot, we are told, looks comic. He is described as "a ridiculous-looking little man. The sort of little man one could never take seriously." In addition to these two, there are a dozen assorted characters of varying classes and nationalities.

At the very beginning of the book and on the first day of the trip, Poirot is speculating with a friend, Monsieur Bouc, over lunch. Bouc has been "studying" the people on board the train, and speaks of it to Poirot:

> "Ah!" he sighed. "If I had but the pen of a Balzac! I would depict this scene." He waved a hand.
>
> "It is an idea, that," said Poirot.

"Ah, you agree? It has not been done. I think? And yet—it lends itself to romance, my friend. All around us are people, of all classes, of all nationalities, of all ages. For three days these people, these strangers to one another, are brought together. They sleep and eat under one roof, they cannot get away from each other. At the end of three days they part, they go their several ways, never perhaps to see each other again."

"And yet," said Poirot, "suppose an accident—"

"Ah, no, my friend—"

"From your point of view it would be regrettable, I agree. But nevertheless let us just for one moment suppose it. Then, perhaps, all these here are linked together—by death."

This leads Poirot to examine rather carefully the thirteen persons on the train, all of whom are dining, and to speculate about them. The fact of the matter is that all of the characters *are* linked together by death—by the various tragedies ensuing from Cassetti/Ratchett's kidnapping of a child, Daisy Armstrong, in America in the distant past. And it is this linking, which is "dangled" before the reader several times in the story, that is the key to solving the mystery.

Let us look at the characters in terms of their relationships. The following list presents some interesting paradigmatic oppositions.

Poirot	twelve murderers on the train	Ratchett
discovers killers	all kill (stab) Ratchett	is killed
refuses to work for Ratchett	all connected to Ratchett and become involved with Poirot	asks Poirot to work for him
looks ridiculous	all look different	looks evil

The puzzle in the story involves discovering how the twelve seemingly random characters on the train are connected. Had Ratchett discerned that they were connected he might have lived. When Poirot discovers they are connected, he finds the murderers—though, curiously enough, he lets them go. He is able to do this because he has been provided (by the murderers) with an acceptable explanation or counterexplanation of the murder, and he chooses to accept this alternative, which involves a mysterious stranger who is described as having left the train after Ratchett's murder.

Once Poirot recognizes that some of the occupants of the train were involved in the Armstrong case, he is able to link all twelve characters together, eventually. Toward the end of the book, but before it is revealed that all twelve occupants of the train are "related," we find the following bit of dialogue:

> "Nothing would surprise me now."
>
> "Nothing! Even if everybody in the train proved to have been in the Armstrong household, I should not express surprise."
>
> "This is a very profound remark," said Poirot.

We do not at this time recognize the significance of this remark, but Bouc has accidentally "stumbled" upon the solution to the mystery, and Christie has him offer it to us, knowing that we will not take it seriously. When we look back, at the end of the story, we discover that Christie has given us all that we needed to know to solve the mystery, but because of our typical "train" of thought, we either neglected or misinterpreted all the clues. That is, we either neglected important signifiers or misinterpreted them and ended up with the wrong signifieds.

DETECTIVES AS SEMIOLOGISTS

Murder mysteries fascinate us because they involve, ultimately, decoding a series of clues—signs and significations (actions, words, objects) that seem random or irrelevant, or both, and that are meaningless until the code, which ties everything together, is found. The great detectives of analytical murder fiction are semiologists, whether they know it or not. And the pleasure we derive from reading mysteries stems, in part, from the semiological problems they pose to us—the "puzzle" that we all try to figure out.

The story in *Murder on the Orient Express* is resolved by seizing upon the fictitious murderer as a means of enabling the real murderers to escape punishment. This resolution is itself connected to certain moral codes we have, such as the notion that evildoers "deserve" to be punished for their crimes and that, in the right circumstances, a sufficiently evil character should be murdered. The dilemma faced by this unusual group of vigilantes (for that's what they were, though some of them were cloaked in European finery) was the dilemma faced by all vigilante groups: How do you justify lawlessness—in this case murder—in the name of law and order? Poirot's response was an emotional one, which may suggest, as psychoanalytic literature so amply demonstrates, that there are forces that move men and women aside from "little gray cells."

The classical murder mystery is a subcategory of the murder mystery genre in which rationality and logic are stressed and in which there is a primal confrontation between the emotion, irrationality, and hatred of the murderer (who must also be extremely devious and calculating) and the mind of the detective. This genre is highly formulaic and has many conventions that must be observed if the mystery is to be legitimate. A good mystery, then, is a confrontation between two minds.

It has been suggested by some Freudian analysts that our fascination with murder mysteries is connected with the desire we all had when we were young to know what was going on in the bedroom, and our frustrations with this problem, which we now transfer to other locked doors and mysterious sounds in the night.

SOCIAL AND POLITICAL DIMENSIONS

Murder on the Orient Express, both the book and the film, may also be examined in terms of its social and political dimensions. The thirteen characters are all linked together, not by that which should join people together—love and a sense of community—but by hatred and death. However, this escape from an alienated and estranged relationship is only momentary. When the Orient Express arrives in France, each person will go his or her separate way, with only the memory of a ritual murder to bind them together.

Ironically, however, the book does suggest the possibility of a society based not upon class differences and estrangement but on a communality of interest—on common goals that all men and women share. The inversion in *Murder on the Orient Express* is interesting because it demonstrates that different classes can work together when they see it is in their interest to do so. Class differences can be overcome.

Of course we must always keep in mind the fact that Cassetti/Ratchett had kidnapped the child of a wealthy family, and it might be argued that the poor and working-class people serve, ultimately, as instruments of the wealthy (and even royal) elements among the murderers. Cassetti/Ratchett had, we know, "touched" the lives of all involved, but it is the insistence, we may presume, of the upper-class people involved that has brought everyone together, remarkably, on the Orient Express. And it is the very existence of social, national, and class differences that everyone counts on to confuse anyone who might be suspicious.

It might be argued that the "mystification" that the murderers create parallels the social mystification that the bourgeoisie finds so important to maintain itself.

A mystery story, in its own way, is a kind of microcosm that parallels the events in society at large. Perhaps it is no accident that so many mysteries—especially the classical English ones involving deduction—involve wealthy and aristocratic elements in society and so few involve "the butler" doing it. This would suggest class conflict too overtly. There are, of course, many mysteries that do have class strife and conflict between the poor and the rich, but many also involve only intra-upper-class murder, a sign of the degeneracy of the bourgeoisie. Ironically, these murders are usually solved by detectives who come from working-class and middle-class backgrounds, so there is still an element of class conflict in these works.

POIROT AS REVOLUTIONARY

In a strange way, then, characters such as Poirot may be said to have a revolutionary dimension, though their efforts are focused on the personal, not the societal, level and they function most immediately as instruments of official bourgeois social morality.

Behind our fascination with the wealthy and their glamourous self-indulgent lifestyles, there is a germ of hostility and resentment and a sense of relative deprivation that has political (and even revolutionary) implications. At the same time, mysteries serve as diversions; they take our attention away from the real world and our problems and offer us characters, many of whom are vile and degenerate, who ultimately pay for their crimes. They function, thus, as sacrificial victims, enabling us to purge ourselves (somewhat) of the hostile feelings we have toward the rich and powerful.

Instead of a real revolution against the real bourgeoisie, in mystery stories we "kill off" the rich, one by one. But it is the imaginary rich we are dealing with and so our hostility (and its revolutionary potential) tends to become dissipated. This might be the ultimate form of mystification, in which imaginary confrontations between a potentially revolutionary proletariat, symbolized by the detective and police, and the bourgeoisie are all acted out in fantasy.

One other thing we learn from mysteries such as *Murder on the Orient Express:* We, the common people, lack the intelligence and wisdom to solve these murders and, by implication, to run our own social and political institutions. We are reduced, psychologically, to children who do not understand what really is going on. The implication of these stories is that we are better off entrusting the control of society to those who are wiser and more powerful than we, which is exactly what the bourgeoisie wants the masses to believe (that is, the status quo is functional).

Although the murder mystery is a commodity manufactured to be sold to the largest possible market, and although the mystery generally acts as an instrument of false consciousness (which distracts people from their real interests), it may also, ironically, have a revolutionary potential. This is because many of the murders found in this genre are committed by members of the upper classes and show the degeneracy of these people. Replacing them, then, seems quite reasonable. The murders also reveal the vulnerability of the upper classes; they cannot be protected from their fates despite their huge homes, servants, and so on. Thus, every murder has political implications and dimensions in spite of itself, and every murderer, without knowing it, helps break the iron grip that the "classes" have upon the consciousness of the "masses."

Many of the murders that take place in these classical mysteries suggest, even if vaguely, the possibility of revolutionary violence and play a role, even if in an oblique manner, in the class struggle. (Actually, in the classical English murder mysteries, the upper class seems to be killing itself off in rapid fashion. Eventually, we may surmise, there will be nothing left but the working class, which will be surprised to discover that the upper class has, bit by bit, destroyed itself, so there is no need for a revolution.)

Agatha Christie would be astonished at such notions. Poirot, of course, would not find them surprising at all.

6

SEVEN POINTS ON
THE GAME OF FOOTBALL

In this chapter, a semiological description of football as a system of signs is suggested, with emphasis on the various sign subsystems (uniforms of the players, officials, dress of the cheerleaders, sign sections in the stands, and related matters). Special attention is given to time and the manipulation of it by teams, and by television broadcasters using the instant replay camera. Attention is then turned to the socializing function of football and its role in preparing people to work in a specialized and bureaucratic society and, in particular, in the corporate world. Football is contrasted with baseball, which is described as a nineteenth-century pastoral game, no longer synchronous with our "hopped up" and time-bound sensibilities. Football is also described, sociologically speaking, as a functional alternative to organized religion. Next a Marxist interpretation of the game is offered, which focuses on its role as a diversion, its treatment of players as commodities, and its business aspects, especially in respect to television advertising.

FOOTBALL IS A GAME OF SIGNS

Football is a very interesting subject for the semiologist because the game is, at once, full of signs and also a signifier of some importance. The stadium is itself one huge sign—a sacred space where enthusiasts (and sometimes fanatics) gather to watch a highly organized, ritualized contest that many have suggested functions as an alternative to war. It is not unusual for 60,000 people or more to gather together for a game, and with television coverage sometimes millions of people watch a game, which means that the entire country "becomes" a football stadium.

Where one sits in the stadium—on the fifty-yard line or way up behind a goalpost—is a signifier of one's wealth or power or status. The field itself is a huge grid, a one-hundred yard rectangle of white lines against brilliant green grass (or Astroturf). The intensity of the colors adds considerably to the excitement of the event and must not be underestimated. On this field are to be seen people in all kinds of different uniforms: the officials in their zebra stripes, the players with their helmets and pads, matching bands, cheerleaders in sweaters and miniskirts, pom-pom girls, coaches with their earphones and electronic paraphernalia, drum majors and majorettes, and many other people. All of these uniforms and trappings are signifiers of the wide variety of skills, activities, and functions taking place at a game: rule enforcement, athletic activity, musical diversion, sexual display, planning and rationality, and so on. Thus a football game is not merely an athletic event but part of a much larger system of events that are connected to the game but which enlarge its significance greatly.

(I have not said anything about the people who attend the games and who frequently wear the colors or emblems of their teams. Sometimes they carry signs. Frequently there are "sign sections" in stadiums and various messages are flashed during halftime, when the bands play and there are various entertainments.)

The game itself is based on signs. Signals are called in the huddles announcing offensive plays. These signals are analogous to what we call "codes," and indicate a precise series of activities that are to be followed at a given point in time. Defensive players learn to watch their opponents for indications that a pass is to be thrown or a certain play is to be run. And a good deal of the game is based on *deception*—that is, giving opponents false signifiers so they will make mistakes. It is the capacity of signs to lie, to give false information, that creates much of the complexity in the game.

The officials also use signs—a variety of gestures that indicate the various penalties to be assessed for violations of the rules. These signals are actually nonverbal, visual metaphors, which enable the officials to indicate to everyone in the stadium the nature of a given transgression. The sign that is most important, the one in which an official stretches both hands over his head to indicate a score, is a signifier with two signifieds: triumph or success for the offensive team and failure for the defensive team, and at the sign, thousands and thousands of people in the stadium (and in the television audience) cheer madly or groan.

While the game progresses there is much activity on the sidelines. In college games bands play rousing songs at certain times to encourage their teams, and cheerleaders lead cheers, jump up and down (displaying their breasts and legs), and carry on, often in rather mechanical dancing and movement displays. Many professional football teams have groups of young and attractive women who "wiggle and jiggle" on the sidelines, indicating that there is a sexual dimension to the game or, more precisely, to the spectacle in which the game is embedded.

INSTANT REPLAY AND THE MODERN SENSIBILITY

As the various subsystems that are part of the spectacle of football work themselves out, there is one sign that is crucial to the understanding of what football means—in its televised form, in particular—and that is the huge scoreboard clock. Time is of the essence in football, but, unlike in baseball and other sports, in football time can be manipulated. And it is this manipulation of time in tightly fought games that leads to the incredible tension generated by the sport.

In a one-sided game there is little tension, and the game often turns into an exhibition of power and competence for the winning team and a study in humiliation for the losing one. But in close games, time is everyone's enemy. The winning team fights to hold on to its advantage and the losing one tries to use what time it has left to best advantage and to score. Many football games are decided in the last minutes and often even in the last seconds of the game. A minute of playing time, because of the rules of the game, can take many minutes of real time.

What further complicates matters, especially in televised games, is the invention of the instant replay, which can show a given play from a variety of different perspectives and which suggests, ultimately, that time doesn't pass the way it does in real life. We keep seeing the past (a given play) over and over again from a variety of angles, so that our sense of continuity and perspective are rendered problematic. Time doesn't pass the way we thought it did and our perspective on the world isn't the only one.

Televised football has become an incredibly sophisticated art form and now closely resembles avant-garde films in that both now simulate stream-of-consciousness thought, which moves backward and forward in time, jumping around almost incoherently at times. Instant replay is vaguely equivalent to the flashback in film, and the invention of instant replay has dramatically altered the nature of televised football (and now other sports as well) in particular, and the modern American sensibility, in general. In Super Bowl XVI, between the San Francisco 49ers and the Cincinnati Bengals, CBS used 16 cameras on the field to televise the game and another 7 for locker room shows and other activities. It had 14 videotape machines for instant replays, which meant that an incredible number of perspectives was possible on every play. Can anyone doubt that a new sensibility arises out of seeing such programming? Or, at least, that a new sensibility is made possible because of the development of such a remarkable kind of program?

FOOTBALL SOCIALIZES US

Football does more than just entertain us. The word "entertain" is like the word "interesting"—neither tells us very much. The questions we should ask about football are those such as: Why do we find football so entertaining? What do we get out of the game? What does it do *for* us (that is, what gratifications does it offer)? What might it be doing *to* us? What does it tell about society?

One very important aspect of football is the way it socializes and enculturates us. It teaches us how to get along in society, what roles to play, what rules to follow, what life is all about, and so on. We are not aware that this is going on most of the time, which means that we are all the more susceptible to the influence of what the game suggests, teaches, and implies. Here we are looking at the game as a signifier of values, attitudes, and beliefs and attempting to ascertain what these signifieds are and what effects they may have upon people (admittedly, a speculative activity).

One thing we learn from examining football is that we live in a highly complex society in which time is critical and communication is important. A good deal of the game involves communication between the coaching staff and the players. Signals are called on both sides for every play. Nothing is done that has not been planned, rehearsed, and prepared over and over again in practice sessions. It is only the fact that people make mistakes, or do things that cannot be anticipated, that messes up the plans of coaches.

In addition, we come to learn that society is highly specialized, and that this specialization functions within group situations. Teams are now made up of offensive and defensive specialists, each with particular talents and abilities. Football teams function as "models" for modern society and we learn, from watching football, that we must be specialists who will work in some highly structured organization, controlled from above (the coaches), and that we must pursue our specialization for the good of the group, first and foremost, and then for ourselves. That's what it means to be a "team player." We learn from football, without being aware of it, that we must prepare ourselves to function in a highly bureaucratic society—most likely within a large corporate entity. Football is "training" for working in the corporate world, and the violence in football becomes transformed into sales campaigns that will "smash" the public or one's competitors or both.

We also learn that specialization and ability constitute a means for upward mobility, especially in professional football, where farm boys, Blacks from working-class families, and others often earn huge salaries. Many youngsters identify very strongly with these football stars, whose heroics on the football field are, at times, quite incredible.

In a sense football is really about containment and breaking free, about order and randomness—though it is always within the context of the game (which is highly structured and rule-dominated). These moments of freedom are exciting and highly exhilarating, but they are fleeting and quite unpredictable. It is not too much of an oversimplification to say that much of football is routine and boring and that what makes the game so exciting is that there are moments when remarkable things happen. Since we can never know when one of these great plays will happen we must pay attention all the time, lest we miss something.

WHY BASEBALL IS BORING

The reason we find football so exciting is that it closely approximates and reflects our contemporary social situation. Football is a twentieth-century sport for people who live in a world in which time is precious (time is money), communication is important (we live in an "information" society), and bureaucratic entities are dominant (corporations, universities, families, and so on). Baseball, on the other hand, is a nineteenth-century pastoral sport in which time is irrelevant, specialization is not crucial, and there is much less reliance on plays and communication. The following list, which contrasts the two sports, is taken from my book *The TV-Guided American:*

Football	Baseball
urban	pastoral
educated players	country boys
time precious	time not important
specialized	general
body contact important	body contact minimal
team effort	individualistic
upsets critical	no upsets
vicarious excitement	relaxation
weekly	daily
spectacle	austere
four quarters with intermission	nine innings, uninterrupted flow
calculation, planning	little strategy
body a weapon	bat as a weapon
small area	large playing area
twentieth century	nineteenth century
territorial	not territorial
team on offense	one player at time on offense

This list offers a set of polar oppositions that reflect the differences between the two sports and their relationship to our character and culture. Baseball is essentially a nineteenth-century sport that is no longer congruent with contemporary American cultural dynamics and thus *seems* terribly slow or "boring" to many people. Baseball games are now events at which to drink beer and relax, and the ambience at baseball games is considerably different from what one finds at football games—especially at crucial games, where ancient antagonisms or a bowl bid hang in the balance.

Our boredom with baseball is a signifier that as a society we have become "hopped up" and thus baseball seems much slower and boring than it used to, years ago. Baseball doesn't offer the gratifications it once did, or, to put it somewhat differently, the gratifications baseball offers don't mean very much to most people any more. Its heroes aren't as important to us as the heroes in football are, it doesn't provide models to imitate or help us gain an appropriate identity the way football does, and it certainly doesn't have the sexual elements in the spectacle surrounding the game that football does.

Baseball still has its attractions and provides many gratifications to people. Some people argue that it is a subtler game than football, which, if true, may be part of the problem. But, for a variety of reasons, it doesn't have the cultural force or resonance that football does, and thus has taken on, inadvertently I would argue, a different role from that of football.

FOOTBALL AS AN ALTERNATIVE TO RELIGION

I have suggested in my discussion of socialization in football that if football's manifest function is to entertain us, its latent function is to socialize us and offer us models to imitate and notions that will help us fit into the contemporary bureaucratic corporate world. I would like to turn now to another aspect of functionalist thought, namely, the notion that some phenomena function as alternatives for other phenomena. My thesis here is that football functions for many people as an *alternative* to religion or, perhaps, that it has a religious or sacred dimension to it that we seldom recognize.

The passionate feelings people have about football (and their teams) and the intensity of our collective interest in the game leads me to think that football has a dimension far beyond that of simply being a sport. Indeed, Michael R. Real in *Mass-Mediated Culture* has written convincingly about the Super Bowl as a mythic spectacle and suggested how, in secular societies, sports "fill the vacuum" left by religions. I would like to suggest here that football—and I will focus on professional football—is in many ways analogous to religion. The following list points out some interesting parallels between the two seemingly different phenomena.

Professional Football	*Religion*
✳ superstars	saints
Sunday game	Sunday service
ticket	offering
great merger	ecumenical movement
complex plays	theology
players on the way to the Super Bowl	knights in search of the Holy Grail
coaches	clergy
stadium	church
fans	congregation

Curiously enough, as religions (especially liberal religions) become more rational and continue to *demythologize* themselves, football becomes more arcane and mysterious, with incredibly complex plays and tactics that function much the way theology does for religion. People seem to have a need for myth, ritual, mystery, and heroism, and football, perhaps more than religion in contemporary societies, is helping people satisfy these needs.

Whether the messages we get from football are as valuable and positive as those we get from sermons and other aspects of religion is another matter, and one that bears thinking about. Has football become "the opiate of the people"? There are some who hold that belief, and it is to their interpretation that we now turn.

THE MARXIST PERSPECTIVE

Football games, held in huge stadiums, with bands, cheerleaders, halftime shows, and so on, are spectacles par excellence. The function of these spectacles (that is, the latent function), it may be argued, is to divert people's attention from their real social situation, to drain them of their emotional energy (which might have been expended on political and social issues), and, ultimately, to convince them of the justness of the political order. A political system that can provide good football is worth keeping. And since football also trains us for our place in the modern, corporate, capitalist world, it is doubly valuable.

The great gatherings of people in America are not (generally) for political purposes, though at times this does happen. Instead we gather together to watch spectacles—of which football is of exemplary importance. It isn't hard to see a parallel between the old Roman principle of bread and circuses—to divert the mobs from their misery—and what goes on in America on Fridays (in high schools), Saturdays (in colleges), and Sundays (in the professional games), as well as Monday nights on television.

Is the intensity of our interest in football a measure of the alienation we feel in our everyday lives—lives in which we sense a radical separation from our possibilities, in which we feel hemmed in by huge bureaucratic structures that dominate our work lives and by the competitiveness that characterizes our social order? The less satisfying our lives, the more bothered we are by the "rat race," the more we turn to vicarious satisfactions like football and, curiously, the less psychic nourishment we get from them. For, ironically, football is itself essentially routine and boring and teaches us, though we generally are not aware of this, that we must learn how to accommodate ourselves to the society in which we live.

Football, especially professional football, is a huge business that exists for one purpose—to make money. It treats players as commodities—objects to be sold and traded, almost at whim (though unionization has modified this a good deal). Players have little sense of loyalty, also. They see the huge profits the owner make and now obtain huge salaries—all that the market can bear. The ultimate irony is that it is television that benefits most from the existence of football, and television uses football for its main purpose—as filler between commercials. Television, as it exists in America, is a business that makes money by selling commercial time. Football attracts large audiences and costs relatively little to produce (compared, say, to a crime show or documentary) so it is very cost-effective.

Thus we have a situation in which everyone is exploiting or trying to exploit everyone else, and the result of all this is that spectacles are produced that are used by people to obtain vicarious excitement and pleasure and that have the hidden functions of teaching people to accept the status quo and to accommodate themselves to corporations and the political order.

The potential for revolutionary violence in the masses is siphoned off as they watch linemen battle one another "in the trenches" and defensive players "hit" halfbacks and cornerbacks. After a weekend of football, the heavy viewer will have participated vicariously in enough violence to fuel a dozen revolutions.

A look at the rosters of football teams shows that Blacks are heavily and disproportionately represented. This is an indication of the fact that Black people suffer more from our economic system than Whites do and thus need football (as well as boxing and other sports) as an instrument of social mobility. For poor Black kids, football is a means of escaping from poverty and achieving middle-class—at least for a while. To be successful, however, one must learn to fit in—to adopt essentially bourgeois values such as being a team player, not causing trouble, doing what one is told, and so on. A player, no matter how talented, who causes "problems" and doesn't follow the rules will not prosper in college or professional football. Thus, there is a price to be paid by players—namely, "accommodation," which leads the way to "co-optation."

FOOTBALL AND THE PSYCHE

I have suggested that football functions as a means of socializing people and of diverting them from paying attention to their real concerns. I would also like to suggest that football is vitally connected with various unconscious processes, which explain, in part, the powerful hold football has on people. If large numbers of people read the comics or watch football or do anything, quite likely it is because there are important psychic gratifications to be obtained, even though people may not be aware of them.

For one thing, there is the matter of violence in football. It is a kind of controlled violence that may satisfy two contradictory desires we have: to be violent and, at the same time, to be controlled so our violence doesn't overwhelm us. This violence is integral to the game, in which there are "blocks," "hits," "tackles," or the like on every play. It stems from a number of sources, such as the fact that we must restrain ourselves from impulsive behavior, and the fact that we are all involved (unconsciously) in Oedipal problems, sibling rivalries, and so on. Quite likely the matter of sexual repression is of primary importance, and the violence becomes a kind of substitute gratification. (There is a connection, also, between violence and eroticism that must be kept in mind. There is a sexual dimension to violence just as there is an aggressive and violent dimension to sexuality.)

The violence in football may also help men with the matter of obtaining masculine identity. We live in an information society, in which processing data and communicating account for a dominant part of the gross national product. In such a society men find it hard to develop a male identity, especially since American male identity has historically been connected to our nineteenth-century lifestyle—cutting wood, herding cattle, doing hard physical labor. Watching violence on the football field becomes one of the few ways in which American men can help themselves form a male identity, even if this violence is vicarious and potentially destructive.

Football lends itself to a number of interpretations of a psychoanalytic nature. For example, we can interpret the game as mirroring the battle between id, ego, and superego forces in the human psyche:

Id	Ego	Superego
offensive team	officials	defensive team
drives	rules	prevention

In this situation, the offensive team wants to have long "drives" and to score; the defensive team wants to stop these drives and get control of the ball; and the officials function as an ego, to keep the game going.

Arnold J. Mandell (1974), a psychiatrist who spent some time with the San Diego Chargers, categorized professional football players as follows:

Position	*Personality Traits*
offensive linemen	ambitious, tenacious, precise, attentive to detail
wide receivers	narcissistic, vain, loners
quarterbacks	self-confident, courageous
defensive linemen	restless, peevish, irritable, intolerant of detail, uninhibited, wild
linebackers	controlled, brutal, internally conflicted

These personality traits are the ones required for people to be able to play their positions, Mandell found. The offensive players, he discovered, keep their lockers neat and orderly, but the lockers of defensive players are invariably messy.

> It became clear that offensive football players like structure and discipline. They want to maintain the status quo. They tend to be conservative as people, and as football players they take comfort in repetitious practice of well-planned and well-executed plays. The defensive players, just as clearly, can't stand structure; their attitudes, their behavior and their lifestyles bear this out. (Mandell, 1974: 12)

All of this is important because more than anything else, Mandell reports, "the game is in the mind," which is probably true of all games.

CONCLUDING REMARKS

Football, though it might seem to be only a simple entertainment, is actually a matter of some consequence from a number of points of view. We use language from football in our political discourse, it creates the lamentable "football widow" every fall, it is played by children, adolescents, college students, and grown men, it is an industry, it has a long history—I could go on and on, endlessly. It is a subject that attracts great attention from the general public and one that deserves attention from the media analyst.

But there is something else to be said here that every media analyst must remember. When we deal with the programs carried by the media—whether we focus on the football, soap operas, news, or any other genre—we must never forget that we are dealing with art forms. And art forms are extremely complicated phenomena. We must be careful that we do not reduce a program to nothing but a system of signs, nothing but a socializing agent, nothing but a means of manipulating people's consciousness, nothing but a subject in which drives, Oedipal problems, and the like are manifested. We must find a way, somehow, to analyze a program from a number of different points of view but also to respect it as a creative effort (perhaps not a very successful one) and a work of art that has performance aspects, aesthetic elements, and more. To be a media analyst one must know all kinds of things and, in a sense, everything at the same time.

7

SEX AND SYMBOL
IN FASHION ADVERTISING

A number of advertisements for cosmetics and fashion are analyzed in this chapter in order to further our understanding of how they generate "meaning" and what they reflect about society. First we deal with advertisements for a cleanser and moisturizer, and a treatment for the entire body, after which we examine an advertisement for Danskins, and finally one for Calvin Klein separates. Attention is paid to the language used in the advertisements and to the way graphics are employed to generate beliefs and attitudes. Semiological techniques are employed to show how language and graphics function as signifiers that are derived from codes we all learn. It is also suggested that advertisements work by "striking" responsive chords in us, and not just by giving us information.

While reading an issue of *Vogue* recently, I noticed that I was, somehow, taken by a number of the advertisements for fashions and cosmetics. Many of these advertisements contained striking photographs and suggestive (and in some cases rather overt) copy. I found myself absorbed by the advertisements. They had a remarkable power over me—to seize my attention and to stimulate, if only for a moment, fantasies of an erotic nature. It was not only the physical characteristics of the models that affected me; rather it was a kind of gestalt effect. There was the element of graphic design, of color, of light, and a host of other matters that "conspired" to excite me.

"What's going on?" I asked myself. That question led me to consider how magazine advertising works to stimulate desire and sell clothes, cosmetics, and everything else that is connected with beauty (in this case) or any product.

In analyzing an advertisement there are a number of factors that we must consider, such as: the ambience, the design, the use of white space, the significant images and symbols, the use of language, the type faces used, and the item itself (and its role and function in society). We can also consider how the advertisements attempts to "sell" us and what roles it offers us to imitate, as well as examine how social phenomena might be reflected, indirectly. (Here I'm thinking about such things as alienation, boredom, conformism, generational conflict, and so on.) We can use whatever concepts we have at our command from history, psychology, sociology, anthropology, and any other disciplines to help us "dissect" the advertisement. In applying all of the above it is important to keep one cardinal principle in mind: The creators of any advertisement are trying to generate some kind of an effect or emotional response. So we must start with the effect and work backwards. What is the fantasy? And how is it induced?

SELLING MAGIC

I will answer these questions by examining some of the advertisements in the April 1978 issue of *Vogue* magazine. I've selected advertisements that, for some reason, caught my attention for a moment and that I think are interesting and worth examining closely.

Let me start with a double-page advertisement by Revlon for its Formula 2 cleanser and moisturizer. The left-hand page of the advertisement is devoted to an extreme close-up of a woman's face, but the face is rendered by using quarter-inch squares of various colors. We are, in fact, given an optical illusion. If we squint, or place the magazine fifteen feet away from us, the squares merge together and form a face. But at arm's length, the face is somewhat distorted and out of focus. It is also larger than life in size. From there we move over to the right-hand page, which has a great deal of white space and is formally designed, approximating axial balance. Generally speaking, large amounts of white space and axial balance (and formality) are associated with quality and "class" in most people's minds.

The copy of the ad stresses science and technology as opposed to nature. We find the following suggestive words and phrases in the advertisement:

Revlon Research Group	precision tip
skincare system	beauty technology
natural electricity	hygiene
formula	principle
skincare that's simple, scientific	

All of these terms are signifiers for science and technology; we are led to think of scientists in laboratories discovering remarkable things that lead to "the New-Face Hygiene" and "beautiful life for your skin." A smaller photograph on this page shows two medicinal-looking bottles, in which the future-age Formula 2 cleanser and moisturizer are packaged.

Though this is something of a generalization, there seems to be a polar opposition in the public's mind that posits a world divided between culture (and with it science and technology) and nature. Thus the people who created the Revlon advertisement had two possibilities: to stress nature and all that's suggested by it, or to stress culture, in this case, science and technology. They chose the latter course and offered their readers a minicourse in science and technology: *This* principle leads to *those* results.

Ultimately what is being sold here—and what is being sold in most cosmetic ads—is magic, and that is where the large rendering of the woman's face comes in. It is an optical illusion that has two functions: First, it catches our attention because when we look at the face we see that it is really only a huge patchwork of squares. At first glance it seems out of focus and strange. But, if we squint or stare at it, magically it becomes a face, just the same way that Revlon Formula 2's "beauty technology of the future" gives you the gift of "life" (for your skin). Just as the law of closure forces us to complete that which is unfinished, we find ourselves obliged to make sense of the picture, and we visualize the woman's face even more completely than we find it. This act of visualization is what is asked of patrons or purchasers of the product. From the bits and pieces of their old faces they are asked (almost forced) to envision the new faces they will have with Formula 2.

Now that the face is taken care of, let us "finish off" the job (the law of closure once again) and take care of the entire body. For this we can use Benandré, which says it "will do for your body what a facial does for your face." This single-page advertisement has, like the Revlon advertisement, axial balance and a considerable amount of white space. It shows a woman in a glass bathtub bathing herself in "Mediterranean blue" water. A bit of greenery signifies the Mediterranean here. The woman's face is clearly shown, in profile, but her body is not. We see only a diffused figure in blue-green water. Benandré promises that its special form of collagen (a protein contained in the connective tissues and bones, which yields gelatin on boiling) helps the body retain moisture and helps it to restore moisture it loses during the day.

This matter of keeping the skin (and body) moist is interesting. A great deal of cosmetic advertising stresses wetness, moisture, and related concepts, as if the body were in danger of becoming an arid desert, devoid of life, dry, uninteresting, and infertile. These ads suggest that women fear, or should fear, losing their body fluids, which becomes the equivalent of losing their capacity to reproduce. This, in turn, is connected with sexuality and desirability. Anxiety over the body as a kind of wasteland is implicit in appeals in advertisements about retaining and restoring moisture. Dehydration is a metaphor for loss of sexual attractiveness and capacity, that is, desexualization.

Dry skin becomes, then, a sign of a woman who is all dried up and who is not sexually responsive—and who may also be sterile. This is because water is connected, in our psyches, with birth. It is also tied to purity, as in baptismal rites when sin is cleansed from a person. All of this suggests that words and images that picture a body of a woman as being dehydrated and losing water have great resonance.

In *Man and His Symbols,* Carl Jung writes:

> Every concept in our conscious mind, in short, has its own psychic associations. While such associations may vary in intensity . . . they are capable of changing the "normal" character of that concept. It may even become something quite different as it drifts below the level of consciousness.

> These subliminal aspects of everything that happens to us may seem to play very little part in our daily lives. But in dream analysis, where the psychologist is dealing with expressions of the unconscious, they are very relevant, for they are the almost invisible roots of our conscious thoughts. That is why commonplace objects or ideas can assume such powerful psychic significance in a dream. (1968: 29)

If we substitute "advertisements" for "dreams" in the above quotation, we can understand why and how we are affected so profoundly by images and words.

The copy in the Benandré ad is full of purple prose indicating power and luxury. Some of the more interesting words and phrases appear below:

lavished	prefer
unique	enriching
expensive	treat yourself
luxury	beneficial
rare oils	beauty treatment

This product is sold as a kind of indulgence for women. The copy hints at sex ("You'll make the skin of your body as nice to touch as the skin on your face. Just ask the one who touches you most."), which is always a strong selling point for beauty aids. But the pictorial element is connected with symbols of innocence—baptism, cleanliness, and so on. And the towel in the lower right-hand corner of the ad is a chaste white. From a psychoanalytic perspective, there is also something regressive about all this. It is almost as if the woman emerges with the skin of a baby. She also is quite undefined sexually; we are certain we are seeing a woman, but her sexuality has been subdued a great deal, which is in keeping with "class" as we have been taught to think of it.

Next let us move on to some clothes for our moist and soft-skinned beauty: Danskins. The advertisement for Danskins shows three female bodies lying down on a blue-green piece of fabric that may also be water—it is hard to say. What is interesting is the arrangement of the bodies, all horizontal and jammed together. Two of the models are lying with their heads on the left and the third is between them with her head to the right side of the picture. Although they touch one another, each seems unaware of any of the others—they all stare off into space in separate directions.

The Danskin ad is extremely simple and formal. It has three elements: a headline, the photograph of the three women, and an element containing six lines of copy, all in capitals. The product advertised is a "freestyle" leotard/swimsuit that comes in various "sensuous styles and colors." The large element of white space contrasts with the crowding in the photograph, a crowding that a Marxist would say reflects a diffuse alienation among the women, who are touching one another but do not seem to be aware of each other. They are all, we must assume, pursuing their private fantasies.

Finally, let us move on to an ad depicting a fully dressed woman in Calvin Klein separates. Here we find a model with her right hand on her hip, her left hand behind her head, and her left knee bent (in the "bashful knee pose") and prominently displayed. The background is gray and there is hardly any text. The shirt the model wears has a plunging neckline, but there is no cleavage showing, and there is a slit in the skirt, which enables her to display her knee.

We are given little textual information: the designer, Calvin Klein; the store where the outfit can be purchased, I. Magnin; and the fabric manufacturer, the Ideacomo group.

The model has long, curly hair. She has a rather cold look on her face, a look that is commonly seen in high-fashion advertising. And she is posed in a way that emphasizes her arms and legs rather than her breasts and hips. Thus attention is focused on her appendages, which are sexually undifferentiated. Yet there is something of a sexually alluring quality about this pose, which shows a lot of upper leg. It may have something to do with the tilt of the hips, the twist of the torso, and the neckline. Perhaps the unnaturalness of the pose is important, also.

BREAKING THE ADVERTISING CODE

The codes of simplicity, white space and formality, appear in the Calvin Klein advertisement just as they did in all the other advertisements discussed to this point. These "couture" codes are learned by people, who are taught, by advertisers, to associate simplicity, spaciousness, and formal structure with "class." In the same manner, we are taught the "meanings" of various typefaces and kinds of images. Soft focus signifies dream-like states, formal structure or design implies "classic" (whatever that means), and so on. All of these associations are carried around in our heads, so that all the advertiser has to do is "activate" us by striking the appropriate responsive chord. As Tony Schwartz (1974: 24-25) writes in *The Responsive Chord:*

> The critical task is to design our package of stimuli so that it resonates with information already stored with the individual and thereby induces the desired learning or behavioral effect. Resonance takes place when the stimuli put into our communication evoke *meaning* in a listener or viewer. That which we put into the communication has no meaning in itself. The meaning of our communication is what a listener or viewer *gets out* of his experience with the communicator's stimulus.

Culture, and "couture," which is part of culture, is a collection of codes we learn that provide us with meaning in the world. But how, specifically, do these codes work, and how do we find meaning in advertisements (as well as other forms of communication)?

In a magazine (or other form of print) advertisement there are two ways that information is communicated—through the text and through pictorial and design elements. We can examine the text to determine what appeals are being pressed forward and what means are used to lead the reader/viewer to desire the product. Anxiety may be provoked. There may be inducements to self-gratifications of varying natures. Snobbery may be invoked. Any number of techniques of persuasion can be used here. And in the pictorial material there is also a "language" that may be employed to generate the desired feelings and fantasies. I have mentioned some of these techniques: design, size, color, grain, focus, and so on. And I have suggested that we learn to associate certain kinds of advertisements with certain kinds of fashions.

Can we take matters a step further? Can we explain how these associations are made and how the various signs and symbols generate the meanings they do? In some cases, yes. To do so we must expand our vocabulary of analysis. I would like to reintroduce some terms from semiology at this point:

metaphor: relationship by analogy
    (example: my love is a red rose)
metonymy: relationship by association
    (example: rich people and mansions)
icon: relationship by resemblance
    (example: photograph of an object)
index: relationship by implication
    (example: smoke implies fire)
symbol: relationship by convention
    (example: Star of David and Jews)

There is a problem in differentiating between metonymy and symbol that I find hard to solve. Neither are motivated or natural, but relationships by association seem to be stronger than relationships by convention. Anything can be a symbol once people learn to accept it as such. But the association between wealth and large mansions seems quite logical. Wealthy people, people with "class," tend to live in large houses, have a great deal of land and space for themselves, and are powerful. Thus spatiality becomes associated with wealth and class indirectly, through the matter of living space found in large homes.

In metonymy, then, the relationships are stronger than in symbols. One important form of metonymy is synecdoche, in which a part stands for a whole or vice versa. Monaco (1977: 135) in *How to Read a Film* suggests that in film "close shots of marching feet to represent an army" is synecdochic and "falling calendar pages" to indicate the passing of time are metonymic, and that it is through metonymy and synecdoche that Hollywood and films in general are able to communicate with people so quickly and powerfully. Thus, for example, sweat is an index of body heat (or nervous anxiety) that functions metonymically since "associated details invoke an abstract idea."

Magazine advertisements function in much the same way, using whatever devices they can to signify "abstract ideas"—what we call signifieds—such as passion, love, romance, and so on. Because these advertisements can use language, they can use metaphor, but more often they also wish to imply or suggest things (fantasies of exotic love, hopes for beauty) through pictorial elements that make use of the devices described above in various combinations.

With these terms we can do more than simply say that signs and symbols work on the basis of associations that people learn and that become codes by which they interpret the world and function in it. For example, let us consider our first advertisement, the one for Revlon's Formula 2 cleanser and moisturizer. Although there are many things going on in this advertisement it seems to me that the most important thing in the ad is the way it forces the reader to turn the optical illusion into a face, which suggests, perhaps subliminally, *magic*. Most cosmetic advertisements involve a belief in magic, but usually the appeals are verbal. In this advertisement, however, we are forced to do a great deal of work, work that "convinces" us that it is logical to believe in magic. Why not? We've just done something magical. We've seen that magic works, with our own eyes.

I see this process as indexical. The Revlon products promise beauty by magic just the way the square patches hold the promise of a face, once we learn how to see the patches correctly. The implication is that Revlon is magic and it will work for you the way your eyes work to figure out the optical illusion. There may also be an element of suggesting that beauty is an illusion and is attainable by all who can employ the correct magic. The picture of the woman in the ad is indexical, but the bottles are symbolic and rely upon the conventional look of medicinal products for their power. The stylishness of the advertisement, with its use of white space and simplicity, is also symbolic. There is nothing natural or logical about our associating white space and simplicity with "class." It is historical, part of our culture, and something that most of us learn.

In the Revlon advertisement and in all advertisements we find a kind of chain reaction taking place. The verbal and pictorial elements in the advertisement function as signifiers that generate feelings and beliefs or signifieds for those who look at and read the advertisement. These feelings and beliefs (and, we might add, hopes, fantasies, and the like) are based on codes (structured belief systems), which, in turn, operate via metaphor, metonymy, icon, index, and symbols in various combinations. Thus, in order to determine how advertisements and other forms of visual-verbal communication generate meaning, we can move beyond the notion of codes and see how the codes themselves function.

It is a fascinating business taking advertisements apart to see how they function and determining what they reflect about society. It is also a perilous business, for there is always the possibility that we are not examining society's fantasies, or those of the creators of the advertisements, but our own. In *The Strategy of Desire,* Ernest Dichter, one of the founding fathers of motivation research, writes:

> Human desire is the raw material we are working with. The strategy of desire is the tool of shaping the human factor, the most important aspect of our worldly arsenal. Human progress is a conquest of the animal within us. No conquest is possible without strategy. (1960: 11)

Whether or not advertising and other tools of persuasion are leading us to higher levels of development is questionable. One thing seems quite evident—knowing the strategies used by the people who work at creating and shaping our desire is important, for then we can make more rational decisions and avoid manipulation. The person who is a slave to fashion is often also a slave to his or her own emotions—emotions that can be manipulated by the fashion advertising industry. But escape is possible.

8

ALL-NEWS RADIO AND THE AMERICAN BOURGEOISIE

In this chapter, all-news radio stations are subjected to a Marxist interpretation. These stations are seen as signifiers of a malaise in American culture, and the dependency that people have on these stations is linked to the American capitalistic economic system, which generates anxiety and thus a need for constant surveillance. The information hunger many people feel is reinforced by the trivial, often commercial, news presented. We then discuss radio commercials, which occupy approximately one-third of each broadcasting hour, and which also generate anxiety and many other negative feelings. Finally, we deal with the audiences of radio talk-show stations and all-news stations, and speculate about what the demographic figures imply.

What are we to make of the various all-news radio stations that we find in many of the "major markets" in America? How do you explain the existence of a station broadcasting news 24 hours a day? One would imagine that all this news would result in incredible overkill or supersaturation; yet the fact is that in San Francisco and in a number of other cities all-news stations exist and are quite profitable.

If you have a radio station that doesn't broadcast music or drama and isn't a talk-show station, what's left, more or less, is "all-news." These stations are highly structured and formulaic: Sports news is broadcast at certain times, business news, the weather reports, features, commentaries, local news, network news—all have more or less regular times, and listeners who are looking for certain kinds of news learn when to tune in and get whatever it is they are interested in.

NEWS AND ALIENATION

The existence of all-news radio stations and now all-news television stations indicates that there is a pervasive "information hunger" that these stations help assuage. But why this voracity for news? Why this need to keep on top of everything? It is a sign (or, to be more precise, semiologically speaking, a signifier) of a widespread and powerful affliction in American culture—an overpowering sense of anxiety and fear (the signified) that tears at the psyches of many people. It also represents a desire to "participate" in history, somehow, even if only vicariously.

Psychoanalysis would describe something like this as a neurosis, a form of behavior that is compulsive, even though it seems quite innocuous (and, perhaps, is even virtuous, since citizens are supposed to be well informed), but which is fueled by relentless and powerful urges that quite likely are harmful. In extreme cases we may even suggest that *"newsaholics" are people who know everything but do nothing*—except listen to (or watch) the news. There may even be something of a desire to be like God in these people—all-knowing, all-pervasive—except that the newsaholic is driven not by a sense of being all-powerful, but by the reverse.

Ultimately, it would seem, the anxiety of the heavy news listener is the product of a sense of powerlessness and insignificance, which means that constant surveillance is necessary. From the Marxist perspective this is quite understandable. Bourgeois capitalist societies generate alienation and a host of afflictions that are connected to it—a sense of powerlessness, insecurity, estrangement, rootlessness, and lack of identity. Because we have no coherent sense of history or ideology, and because we live in a society that may be described as "dog-eat-dog," we must, if we are to survive, keep on top of things and never be caught napping.

Our capacity to absorb enormous amounts of programming on all-news stations is tied to this anxiety and to something else (to continue the Marxist critique): What we are offered is not really news but essentially trivia—sensational "junk food for the mind" that does not deal seriously with our social and political problems but that instead diverts and entertains us. Because this so-called news is so insubstantial, we are able to devour huge quantities of it and never get full. We lack a well-defined and coherent political sensibility that would enable us to make sense of events. All we get, for the most part, is "figure" divorced from "ground," that is, a succession of reports on all kinds of things—fires, crimes, political events, film reviews, food tips, and the weather—that all occupy the foreground.

This "news" is all superficially interesting and satisfies our curiosity, but it doesn't help us to orient ourselves because nothing fits together with anything else. The pressure within the news media to cover events as they happen, to get the news first—this prevents analysis and backgrounding from taking place. "To the blind, all things are sudden," someone once said, and to those with no sense of history and social relations, with no understanding of the causes of events and the implications of what happens, all-news stations are literally sensational. What we get may be fascinating but it is not particularly edifying or useful to the listener who wishes to uncover the meaning of events.

Frequently media scholars distinguish between "hard news" and "soft news." Hard news is supposedly serious; it deals with important events in the social, political, and economic arenas. But much of what we get in these areas is really the product of the public relations mills of various political leaders, governmental agencies, businesses, or other organizations. The news reporters are, as a rule, highly moral and responsible professionals who do the best they can to avoid being manipulated, to offer accurate information, and so forth, but they have, without recognizing it, adopted the establishment's point of view, and their ideas are, as Marxists would put it, "the ideas of the ruling class."

NEWS AND RULING-CLASS IDEOLOGY

A study of televised news conducted in Great Britain reached some conclusions about the role of broadcasters in the presentation of ideology:

> News talk occurs within a cultural framework which stresses balance and impartiality. Yet despite this, detailed analysis reveals that it consistently maintains and supports a cultural framework within which viewpoints favourable to the *status quo* are given *preferred* and *privileged* readings.

> This representation of events as news is not governed by a conscious attempt to present ideology. The journalists and producers and those

they allow to broadcast of course believe that their routines and codes merely serve to fashion the news into intelligible and meaningful bulletins. (Glasgow University Media Group, 1980: 122)

The ideological assumptions, made by newscasters are not generally recognized, either by the news people or their audiences. That makes them all the more insidious. The news professionals select items to focus attention on from a huge inventory of what is available. Their selection of items for broadcast (along with the lack of backgrounding) is crucial. What is neglected? What is not seen as worth dealing with? What has little news value? Those are some questions we might ask as we consider the adequacy of the news diet we get on all-news stations. It is possible that some stories that might be of considerable significance are neglected or just mentioned in passing because of the unconscious assumptions of the news editors and audiences of these news programs, who have been taught over a number of years what is important and what isn't. Some issues, by their nature, are harder to uncover or more complicated to analyze; they are often passed over by editors and reporters facing the pressures of limited time and money.

When we get to soft news—features of one sort of another—we find an insidious commercialization present in most of them, for they almost always contain, as an end result, the promotion of some product or service. We learn about "undiscovered" restaurants, interesting films, and the best boutiques in which to buy this or that kind of clothing. Ultimately, though these features may seem quite innocent, they serve as free advertisements for businesses.

From the sociological perspective, the manifest functions of these features are to entertain and to provide useful information; the latent function is to "sell" restaurants, movies, and all manner of other things. To the Marxist, hard news and soft news are more or less the same; they help support the ideological perspectives of the ruling classes and they fuel the engines of consumption.

COMMERCIALS AND ANXIETY

The most important engines of consumption in radio broadcasting are the commercials; about *16 to 18 minutes of every hour—roughly one-third of broadcast time—is devoted to commercials.* Thus one-third of the information broadcast on all-news stations is product news. When we add soft news to this, we find that a very large block of news air time is actually given to commercial information. In addition, most of the imagination, intelligence, and creativity found on radio—and in popular culture in general—is lavished on commercials. This is because they are what is most important; they are the "raison d'être" for the stations, which, after all, are businesses that exist to make money through the use of the public airwaves.

We are bombarded with slogans, jingles, and announcements that use whatever subliminal or other persuasive techniques are available to make us feel anxious about ourselves, to generate feelings of relative deprivation, and to get us to *buy* something (see Chapter 7 for more on the power of advertising). Ironically, to assuage our bad feelings, to rid ourselves of these anxieties about ourselves and our situation, we turn to media—movies, soap operas, music, or even all-news radio stations—*which reinforce the very problems we hope they will help us solve*. Thus we become caught in a vicious cycle from which there is no escape. The more we listen to the news (and the ubiquitous commercials), the unhappier we get, and the unhappier we get, the more we listen to the news.

When we listen to all-news radio stations, especially for long periods of time, we seldom can avoid ending up disturbed. We become anxious about the world and plagued by various negative emotions. Small wonder that the average person listens to all-news stations in only 20- or 30-minute segments and then switches to other stations. This may explain why, in certain circumstances, no news is good news.

CAUGHT IN THE MIDDLE

Demographic studies of the audiences of all-news programs indicate that listeners tend to be "up-scale," that is, affluent professional types who are well educated and, it would seem, far removed from the pathetic figures I have described. Trendy affluents most certainly are not tense, anxiety-ridden souls endlessly searching for security and desperate about keeping abreast of things lest they be caught unawares. Or are they?

Do all of these "up-scale" people have a real sense of security and a well-defined identity? Or is there, perhaps, a faint tinge of desperation showing in the way they follow the business news or listen to the features to be told the "right movies, the "right" restaurants, and the "right" opinions to have about all kinds of things.

News listeners tend to be middle-class people. Those in the proletariat (who live in poverty) have relatively little interest in the news. These people tend to be fatalists who are unable to change the system that oppresses them; they are generally uninvolved and unconcerned (except in cases immediate to their interests) about events in the world. Those in the upper classes own the means of production—including the media—and need not worry too much about what is going on. They control the events. Older people also don't worry much about what is going on in the world (aside from issues dealing with social security and related matters) and, instead, listen to talk-shows in large numbers. Approximately half of the audience of radio talk-shows is composed of people over 65 years old. Young people are busy listening to music stations and worrying about such age-related problems as acne, sex, fashion, cars, and love. When we shear off the relatively old, the very young, the poor, and the rich we are left with the middle- (and post-teen- and pre-middle-) aged, middle-class people who are the prime customers of all-news programs.

The members of this group have the most to gain or to lose from the tide of events. They have no power to alter the system set up by the upper classes—nor do they have the desire to. They have been thoroughly indoctrinated by the ideology fed them day and night on their radios and through the other media and hope only to improve their situation so that someday they may join the upper class they have tried so long to emulate. But this requires constant attention to the news if they are to maintain their current status and possibly some day get the edge on their competitors—other middle-class people much like themselves. These people, according to Marxist, are the guilt-ridden victims of all-news radio.

EPILOGUE:
SHMOOS AND ANALYSIS

A number of years ago, when I was about to enter graduate school to work on a doctorate in American studies, my brother, Jason, suggested I not bother. "American studies is like a Shmoo," he said. [For those who don't know what Shmoos are, let me explain. They are mythical creatures that love more than anything else to do things for people, including offering themselves as food. Fried, they taste like steak; baked, like ham; roasted, like roast beef. Their whiskers can be used for toothpicks and their skin for leather. And they multiply like crazy. They are the invention of Al Capp, and they appeared in *Li'l Abner*—one of the most important comic strips ever produced in America.]

"American studies is like a Shmoo. If you bake it you're a historian, if you fry it you're a literary critic, if you boil it you're a sociologist, if you broil it you're a political scientist."

We can apply this insight to analysis, for critics and media analysts don't just exist; they always have a point of view. Or, with eclectic analysts, several points of view. And they bring their point (or points) of view, their sense of the world, their understanding of people and society to whatever it is that they analyze. Analysis, at least as I see things, doesn't just exist in and of itself.

I have selected four techniques that I consider to be of great importance, but there are other techniques I could have dealt with. The room in which our four critics sat watching that episode of *Dallas* could have been crowded with people. There might have been a literary critic, who would have been concerned with such matters as plot, theme, point of view, motivation of characters, setting, tone, and so on. There might have been a "myth-ritual-symbol" critic, with an anthropological background, with what might be described as "culturological" interests. An ethical critic might have focused upon moral problems raised in the episode and other philosophical concerns, while an aesthetically oriented critic might have been concerned with such aspects of the production as lighting, camera angles, kinds of shots, fades, cutting, sound effects, and so on. Jungian critics would look for archetypes, shadows, anima and animus figures, heroes, trickster figures, and that kind of thing. Experts in nonverbal behavior might examine the program in terms of the facial expressions of the characters (especially in close-ups), their body language, and a host of similar concepts.

The goal of media analysis, as I see things, is to offer the most comprehensive, most interesting, most profound reading of a text possible. Some people think that analysis is a waste of time and that it "destroys" a work. This is a "know-nothing" position that assumes that the more mindless our response to a television program or film (or whatever), the better off we are.

I would argue that we need analysis to fully appreciate and understand a work. Furthermore, creative artists of all kinds (and in all media) need to be self-critical—in the positive sense of the term—so that they can understand how they generated the effects they were after, what worked and what didn't. You need theory in order to be able to practice successfully and effectively; otherwise the successes you have are just the results of accidents and luck. Just as creative people are generally also very analytical, analysts are often also very creative. I hope that this volume has provided some encouragement for others to combine analysis and creativity.

REFERENCES

Bakhtin, M. M. (1981). *The dialogic imagination* (edited by Michael Holquist; translated by Caryl Emerson & Michael Holquist). Austin, TX: University of Texas Press.

Berger, A. A. (1976). "Culture-codes." (mimeo)

Bettelheim, B. (1977). *The uses of enchantment: The meaning and importance of fairy tales.* New York: Vintage Books.

Brenner, C. (1974). *An elementary textbook of psychoanalysis.* Garden City, NY: Doubleday.

Caudwell, C. (1971). *Studies and further studies in a dying culture.* New York: Monthly Review Press.

Culler, J. (1976). *Structuralist poetics: Structuralism, linguistics and the study of literature.* Ithaca, NY: Cornell University Press.

Dichter, E. (1960). *The strategy of desire.* London: Boardman.

Dichter, E. (1964). *Handbook of consumer motivations: The psychology of the world of objects.* New York: McGraw-Hill.

Dressler, D. (1969). *Sociology: The study of human interaction.* New York: Knopf.

Eco, U. (1972, Autumn). "Towards a semiotic inquiry into the television message." *Working Papers in Cultural Studies, 3.*

Eco, U. (1976). *A theory of semiotics.* Bloomington: Indiana University Press.

Eidelberg, L. (1968). *The encyclopedia of psychoanalysis.* New York: Macmillan.

Enzenberger, H. M. (1974). *The consciousness industry.* New York: Seabury.

Freud, S. (1962). *Civilization and its discontents.* New York: W. W. Norton.

Freud, S. (1963). *Character and culture* (P. Rieff, ed.). New York: Collier.

Fromm, E. (1957). *The forgotten language: An introduction to the understanding of dreams, fairy tales and myths.* New York: Grove.

Fromm, E. (1962). *Beyond the chains of illusion: My encounter with Marx and Freud.* New York: Simon & Schuster.

Glasgow University Media Group (1980). *More bad news.* London: Routledge & Kegan Paul.

Grotjahn, M. (1966). *Beyond laughter.* New York: McGraw-Hill.

Haug, W. F. (1986). *Critique of commodity aesthetics: Appearance, sexuality and advertising in capitalist society.* Minneapolis: University of Minnesota Press.

Hinsie, L. E., & Campbell, R. J. (1970). *Psychiatric dictionary.* New York: Oxford University Press.

Horton, P., & Hunt, C. (1972). *Sociology.* New York: McGraw-Hill.

Jung, C. (1968). *Man and his symbols.* New York: Dell.

Katz, E., Blumler, J. G., & Gurevitch, M. (1979). "Utilization of mass communication by the individual." In G. Gumpert & R. Cathcart (eds.), *Inter/Media.* New York: Oxford University Press.

Lazere, D. (1977, April). Article in "Mass culture, political consciousness and English studies." Special issue, *College English, 38.*

LeFebvre, H. (1984). *Everyday life in the modern world.* New Brunswick, NJ: Transaction Books.

REFERENCES

Lesser, S. (1957). *Fiction and the unconscious*. Boston: Beacon.

McLuhan, M. (1967). *The mechanical bride*. Boston: Beacon.

Mandell, A. J. (1974, October). "A psychiatric study of professional football." *Saturday Review/World*.

Marx, K. (1964). *Selected writings in sociology and social philosophy* (T. B. Bottomore & M. Rubel, eds.). New York: McGraw-Hill.

Monaco, J. (1977). *How to read a film*. New York: Oxford University Press.

Propp, V. (1968). *Morphology of the folk tale*. Austin: University of Texas Press.

Saussure, F. de (1966). *Course in general linguistics*. New York: McGraw-Hill.

Schwartz, T. (1974). *The responsive chord*. Garden City, NY: Doubleday.

Tucker, R. C. (ed.) (1972). *The Marx-Engels reader*. New York: W. W. Norton.

Williams, R. (1977). *Marxism and literature*. Oxford: Oxford University Press.

NAME INDEX

SUBJECT INDEX

ABOUT THE AUTHOR

ARTHUR ASA BERGER is Professor of Broadcast Communication Arts at San Francisco State University, where he has taught since 1965. He has written extensively on popular culture, the mass media, and related concerns. Among his books are *Scripts: Writing for Radio and Television, Agitpop: Political Culture and Communication Theory, Seeing Is Believing,* and *Media USA.*

Dr. Berger had a Fulbright scholarship to Italy where he taught at the University of Milan. He has lectured extensively on media and popular culture—in Denmark, Norway, Sweden, and Finland as a guest of the Nordic Institute of Folklore; in Greece, Lebanon, and Turkey in 1973 and in Brazil in 1987 for the United States Information Agency; and in Germany, France, the People's Republic of China, and England at the request of various universities and institutions. He is a Consulting and Contributing Editor for the *Journal of Communications,* Film and Television Review Editor for *Society* magazine, editor of a series of reprints, "Classics in Communications" for Transaction Books, and a consulting editor for *Humor* magazine. He has appeared on *20/20* and the *Today* show, and appears frequently on various local television and radio stations in the San Francisco area.

He is married to Phyllis Wolfson Berger, who teaches philosophy at Diablo Valley College, and has a daughter, Miriam Beesley, who is a scriptwriter, and a son, Gabriel Berger, who is working on a Ph.D. in mathematics at Columbia University.

NOTES

NOTES

NOTES